Bio-deterioration of Museum Materials

Bio-deterioration of Museum Materials

Dr. S.M. Nair

(Former Director, National Museum of Natural History, New Delhi)

AGAM KALA PRAKASHAN

DELHI

First Published 2011

ISBN : 978-81-7320-110-3

Published by:
Dr. Agam Prasad, M.A., Ph.D., Diploma in Museology
For Āgam Kala Prakashan
34, Central Market, Ashok Vihar
Delhi - 110 052
Tel.: 011-27212195, 65688806-7
Fax: 91-11-27212195
Email: agambooks@gmail.com, agambook@yahoo.com
www.agamkala.com

Composed by:
Aman Printographics
Delhi - 110 052
Mobile: 9891395309

Printed by:
Chawla Offsets
Delhi-110 052

Printed in India

PREFACE

This book on the Biodeterioration of museum materials is the result of the research work I have done for my Ph.D. at the Department of Museology of the M.S. University of Baroda and the refrerence studies undertaken at the Smithsonian Institution, Washington D.C. and the International Biodeterioration Research Centre at Birmingham, U.K. I was initiated in to this study by my brother, Dr. K.S.S. Nair when he as a Lecturer at the Dept. of Zoology, M.S. University of Baroda by making me interested to study the biology and feeding habits of dermestid beetles which are serious pests of museum collections.

Further encouragement and guidance for this study was received from Dr. O.P. Agrawal former Director, National Research Laboratory for Conservation, Lucknow and ex-Director INTACH Conservation Center, New Delhi. No studies on biodeteriorahon of cultural property in India were available and as much this was a pioneering effort in this field. I made an extensive visit of museum collections in India, both on display and storage to locate, identify and study fungi and insects that bring about deterioration of museum objects. The samples of fungi and insects collected were cultured in the laboratory to understand their feeding habits, nature of damage done to objects and the control measures required to eliminate them. Various chemical formulations of repellents and insecticides were used to arrive at the lethal doses required to control them which at the same time will have no deleterious effect on the object and least toxic to humans.

The book is divided in to seven chapters. These include organisms responsible for biodeterioration, feeding responses of some insect pests, and the wise use of insecticides, and fungicides. Extensive references to literature are also provided.

It is hoped that the book will be found useful by museum curators, conservators and other custodians of cultural property as well as students of museology and conservation. The author will be grateful for any suggestions, comments and conrtructive criticism to improve the quality fo the book in future editions.

The encouragement and help I received from my wife, Leela Nair, my daughters Meena and Divya and my son in laws Mr. E.K. Nareshwar and Mr. Sai Ram Nagpal have gone a long way in seeing this work to its completion.

(S.M. Nair)

H-1C, Saket,
New Delhi-110 017

3 March, 2011

CONTENTS

Chapter I

INTRODUCTION

Museums are institution that preserve objects representing the cultural and natural heritage of mankind. The scope of a museum today, however, has grown beyond the limiter concept of accumulating and preserving antiquities, works of art, ethnographic materials and natural history specimens. It nc more is concerned only with man and his creations past or present, but with the whole world its physical cultural and natural environment. Each museum confines itself to a specific area within this immense variety of materials and knowledge. We thus have museums of Art, Archaeology Anthropology, Science and Technology, Natural History, Handicrafts and so on. The scope of a contemporary has become more varied and diverse both in content and quality as well as in the educational services they offer to the public.

This change in the status and relevance of the museum is indicative of the evolutionary process undergone by those which have adapted and changed to meet the needs of the modern society. Those which have not, still remain as 'glorified warehouses' of the past. The latter are important too because they hold valuable collections, irrespective of the extent to which they enlighten the visitors, and also because they abound in number. With the increasing complexity of the collections housed or used in museums, the problem of preserving them and of holding the factors responsible for their deterioration at bay have become further complex.

Deterioration of materials is an inescapable phenomenon in any given space or time. It is in fact part of the whole natural process of recycling matter. Preservation of materials therefore involves a constant fight against the natural forces of deterioration, such as physical, chemical and biological factors affecting materials. Museums have the responsibility of preserving their holdings. Yet this important aspect of museum function is not receiving the attention it deserves. Much of the deterioration that is taking place in museums is the result of a lack of awareness of the seriousness of the problem and consequent neglect on the part of the custodians themselves. As aptly pointed out in "America's Museums – the Belmont Report", "It is questionable whether even a small percentage of museums are doing anything more than presiding over the steady deterioration of that which they have been instituted to preserve". This is true of many museums all over the world. Custodians of museum collections must realize the responsibility that rests on them in the conservation of the cultural and natural heritage – a responsibility towards the present and future generations of mankind transcending all national barriers. The conservators, curators, directors and all those in charge of museum collections should continuously review whether they are giving the best possible care for the protection of their holdings against the forces of deterioration.

Fortunately today, there is a growing awareness about the importance of conservation of cultural property. Conservation laboratories in museums are trying to apply modern scientific knowledge to the protection of materials. There are also national and international organisations committed to the advancement and coordination of conservation efforts. But these benefits do not seem to rearch many museums, whether in developing or developed countries. Most museums still do not have a regular conservation facility. Museum curators often lack basic knowledge of the factors responsible for the deterioration of materials and of elementary methods of conservation.

One of the major factors responsible for deterioration of materials is the deleterious effects brought upon objects by the activities of living organisms like fungi and insects. This process, called 'biodeterioration', is a problem of considerable significance in tropical humid regions of the world. The purpose of this book is to provide an overview of the principal organisms responsible for biodeterioration, the nature of damage caused by them and the preventive and control measures that can be applied to protect museum materials.

Though rapid strides have been made in the general field of conservation dealing with physical and chemical aspects of deterioration of museum materials, the problem of biodeterioration of materials does not seem to have received enough attention. The influence of living organisms on materials, in a broad sense, brings about changes that may be desirable or undesirable. Desirable changes on materials through the activities of organisms is the subject matter of technical or industrial microbiology, economic, entomology, etc. Most of the undesirable changes lead us to the study of biodeterioration.

Biodeterioration of materials can be defined as "any undesirable change in the structure and properties of materials caused by the vital activities of living organisms" (Hueck, 1968). This covers a wide field of study. In nature, biodeterioration, to a large extent, is a desirable phenomenon, such as in the case of the decomposition of dead plants and animals by bacteria, breaking them down to their basic elements. Such decomposition of dead biological matter ensures the continuance of life on earth, as otherwise all dead animals and plants would pile up and life would have come to a standstill. We, however, have to fight the forces of deterioration to preserve certain objects and materials. A wide range of materials of economic importance in agriculture, engineering and manufacturing industries are susceptible to biological deterioration. Considerable progress has been made in recent years to protect and preserve such materials. The prevention of biodeterioration of museum materials, however, has not received similar attention.

Today Museum curators and conservators are aware that several kinds of fungi, insects etc. destroy museum material and that it is necessary to devise suitable control measures. But, the nature and extent of deterioration brought about by different organisms, their exact identity, ecology, feeding habits, resistance to toxicity and the effective lethal range of biocides required for their extermination have not been fully understood. Any systematic attempt at controlling the problems of biodeterioration have to be largely based on an adequate knowledge of the organisms themselves. Consider for example the problem of insect pests in museums. In the case of many of these pests it the larvae and not the adults that are actually harmful to the materials. Extermination of adult insects in such cases would not solve the problem. The feeding habits of insects vary considerably necessitating the application of stomach poisons, contact poisons or respiratory poisons as may be required. Most museum pests have remarkable abilities to survive unfavourable conditions and to hide and protect themselves from being detected some pests are resistant to certain biocides whereas others are not. Such basic information, therefore, is essential for an intelligent application of control measures. Identification of the organism is the key to the kind of damage that may be expected. Maintaining the attitude that "an insect is an insect and that it makes no difference what kind it is because we kill them all anyway" is a sure sign that the control measures will fail to give any thing but temporary relief, if at all.

The type of biological destruction suffered by an object depends upon two basic factors, namely, the material composition of the object and the particular organism that has affected it. These two aspects are always interlinked. Any one insect may not attack all kinds of material as each insect has its own food preference. A pest of wool does not feed on cotton, and a wood boring beetle does not attack leather. An understanding of the chemical composition of the material and its relation to possible biological activity, therefore is another aspect of basic significance in the study of biodeterioration.

All organic materials are susceptible to biodeterioration of one form or the other. These materials, being biological in origin, are either plant products made up of cellulosic substances containing complex carbohydrates or of animal matter built up of protein substances. Insect pests have preferences either for cellulosic materials or for proteinaceous substances, though some feed on both.

Yet another factor of basic importance to biodeterioration is the availability of favourable environmental conditions, particularly that of suitable temperature and humidity conducive to the growth and development of the organisms in question. As mentioned earlier, favourable conditions are available almost all the year round in tropical humid regions. A survey of museum collections conducted in India showed the existence of a large variety of fungal and insect species deleterious to objects. Similar conditions can be expected in other countries of Asia, South America, Africa, and Auistralia. Reports of the types of museum pests found on some of these continents are available. Accounts of biodeterioration in temperate areas of the world such as Europe, United Kingdom, North America, Russia etc. are also available. However, most of these contain information from isolated studies conducted here and there. A comprehensive study of the biological agents responsible for the deterioration of museum materials in each region is desirable.

No systematic account of the biodeterioration of museum materials in India is available. This book is an attempt of fill this lacuna.

Symptoms of Biodeterioration

Damage recognition and identification of the organism responsible is the key to successful control measure. In the case of insects, the surest way of identifying the pest is to examine adult specimens. In several cases the species can be identified from larvae, but not always. Adults, live or dead, larvae or their cast skins, and pupae or pupal exuviate, could often be of help in identifying the type of organism responsible for the damage.

Pests that leave such evidence on material include several of the beetles and moths. Some pests may not be found on the damaged materials or even in the immediate vicinity. Usually the insect is in hiding or has left to feed elsewhere. These pests can also be identified with the help of secondary evidences, such as the type of damage done on the object Damage done by wood borers, termites, silverfish and certain species of dermestid beetles can be identified from the characteristics of the damage.

Detection of the cause of damage, after the pest has left, is a complex phenomenon. Some damage can be identified at a glance, but in other cases, more careful examination may be necessary. Pests can also be determined from evidences such as faecal pellets, scales, cast skins, webbings or hairs. Quite often exit holes made by insects on an object provide the clue to their identity. Taking careful note of all these factors, makes it often possible to identify the pest and to adopt the most suitable control measures.

Museum personnel responsible for the care and preservation of objects and exhibits should be able to recognize the symptoms of biodeterioration. The following table lists some of the common symptoms of damage or evidence of the activity of the organisms responsible.

Symptoms of biodeterioration	*Examples*
Stains and discolourations	Surface growth of fungi on paper, leather, textiles, causing stains and discolouration.
Leisons	Parts of the material eaten or broken away as in damage to paper by silver fish, cockroaches or rodents.
Disfigurement	Positive changes in the structure of a painting due to fungus attack, disfigurement of stone due to lichen growth or of wall paintings due to algal growth.

Pitting	Pitting corrosion of iron objects under exceptional circumstances, associated with sulphure reducing bacteria.
Tunnelling	Tunnels bored into book-bindings by book-worms or into wood by wood borers.
Fibrillization	Loss of coherence in fibrous materials, as in wool attached by micro-organisms.
Penetrations	The invasion of the lumen of certain natural fibres by fungi or of wood by dry-rot fungi.
Changes in mechanical properties.	Loss of weight and strength of dry-rot wood or reduction of breaking strength of cotton fibres or paper attacked by fungi.
Changes in Chemical Properties.	Breakdown of cellulose by micro-organisms, foxing on paper.
Detachment of fibrous parts.	Falling of hair from stuffed mammalian specimens or detachment of fibrous parts from upholstered furniture due to attack by dermestid beetles.
Powder/granule formations.	Ejection of faecal pellets in the form of small granules or powder from wood through small holes by wood borers inside.
Development of odour	As in the mildewing of paper.

The above symptoms should be considered as possible clues to the type of bio-deterioration suffered by on object. The determination of the exact cause and the causative agents, however, cannot depend only on such clues and would call for details scientific studies.

Chapter II

ORGANISMS RESPONSIBLE FOR BIODETERIORATION

Several species of living organisms bring about deterioration of museum materials. Fungi, insects and rodents are the most common. Bacterial decay also takes places under exceptional circumstances. As far as buildings, monuments and historical structures are concerned, there is the problem of damage caused by algae, lichens, liverworts, mosses and even higher plants. Damage recognition and identification of the causative agent are necessary for adopting successful control measures. This involves some basic biological knowledge about the organisms concerned. In the absence of such knowledge problems of biodeterioration may not be understood or recognized properly. It is also necessary to understand biological factors causing deterioration as distinct from the non-biological ones. Preventive and curative treatments must be based on the correct diagnosis of the problem. A general account of the biological agents responsible for the deterioration of museum objects is given in this chapter.

Disfigurement and damage caused by bacteria, fungi, algae, lichens and moss to different kinds of materials have been studied and described by many investigators. Of particular significance to museum collections is the destruction brought about by fungus growth on organic materials like wood, paper, leather, textiles and the like. This is a common problem with organic materials if adequate precautionary measures are not taken. Bacterial attack on museum objects can take place under certain circumstances. Algae, moss and lichens are more of a problem to monuments exposed to the weather and stone sculptures exhibited outdoors.

BACTERIA

Normal conditions of temperature, humidity and light obtainable in museums do not favour bacterial growth on any organic material. As an exception to this, mention must be made of possible bacterial attack on zoological specimens if the process of their preservation is either delayed or defectively done. Bacterial attack resulting in irreparable loss and damage to materials such as textiles, paintings manuscripts, leather, wooden objects and biological specimens may also occur in cases where a flood submerges the collections as has happened in Florence, Italy and in some museums in India. This, of course, is not a normal situation. All the same, the conservation scientist cannot afford to overlook such an eventuality and the need to equip himself for dealing with it.

Bacteria occur in soil, water and air. They require the presence of water for their growth and prefer wetter situations than what are needed by fungi. A number of bacteria are aerobic i.e., they require oxygen for growth; some are anaerobic, i.e., they grow in the absence of oxygen; and some other are facultative anaerobes, living either in the presence or absence of oxygen. Bacteria are extremely minute, usually 5 to 10 microns in length and are relatively simple unicellular organisms belonging to the class Schizomycetes. Each kind of bacterium is adapted physiologically to survive in particular habitats.

Bacterial attack on frescoes has been reported by Tonolo Antonio *et. al.* (1963) in Italy. The growth of bacteria is said to have caused serious changes on the picture surfaces resulting in the loss of original colour. Large bacterial colonies of the coccus type belonging to the species *Sarcina lutea* are the ones reported by them. Fausta Gallo (1963) isolated some forms of *Eubacteri* belonging to the genus *Cellvibrio,* and Cellfacicula as well as *Myxobacteria* belonging to the genus *Cytophaga* from paper showing appreciable cellulose dissolving activity.

The protein-tannin complex of leather is occasionally attacked by bacteria in extremely humid conditions. A large variety of bacteria associated with the destruction of paper have been studied by many investigators. Although aerobic bacteria may be involved in the deterioration of paper, they do not play a predominant role as do the fungi. According to Waksman (1940), aerobic cellulose decomposing bacteria belong to four distinct groups: (i) *Cytophaga*, ii) *Cellvibrio*, iii) *Cellfacicula* and iv) *Myxobacteria* which agrees with the observations of Fausta Gallo cited above. Bacterial decomposition brings about staining, tendering and loss of strength to the materials affected.

In the corrosion of certain metals, particularly iron, a kind of bacteria known as 'Sulphate – reducing bacteria' plays an important role. These bacteria are occasionally present in water that is very low in oxygen and which contains sulphates and organic matter. In such cases Hydrogen Sulphide results as a bye-product of bacterial reduction. In contact with iron, the Hydrogen Sulphide froms Ferrous Sulphide. The bacteria which cause underground corrosion of iron obtain Hydrogen from cathodic surfaces, thus permitting the corrosion reaction to continue.

Roger Heim *et. al.* (1968) report the presence of thio-bacteria, silico-bacteria and nitrifying bacteria among the micro-organisms that attack monuments and buildings of stone. Many of these are capable of transforming nitrates into nitrites and sulphates into sulphides, thus playing predominant roles in the complex process of the biodterioration of stone.

ALGAE

Algae too, generally can not grow under museum conditions as they need plenty of water and sunlight for growth. They contain chlorophyll, unlike fungi, and carry on photosynthesis. Some algae are unicellular whereas others are multi-cellular and colonial. They are found in a great variety of habitats, the vast majority in water. They also occur in moist soil, rocks and walls.

As far as the biodeterioration of cultural property is concerned, it may be said that sculptures, monuments and wall paintings exposed to weather in highly humidity conditions are the only ones susceptible to algal damage. Antonio Tonolo *et.al.* (1963) have reported the presence of algae belonging to the group of *Chlorophyceae* on frescoes exposed to conditions of high humidity (above 95%) bringing about visible changes on the painting in the form of different tones of green and black stains. Roger Heim (1968) reports that the micro-organisms that attack monuments and buildings of stone include some algae belonging to *Chlorophyceae* such as *Pleurococcus* and *Cyanophyceae* such as *Scytonema, Tolypothrix, Gloecapsa, Chlorogles* and *Porphyrosiphon.*

FUNGI

Fungi play important role in the biodeterioration of materials. They differ fundamentally from green plants in their lack of chlorophyll. They are unable to synthesise their own food and are therefore, either saprophytic (i.e., feeding on dead organic matter) or parasitic. Though some fungi are whitish, others after green, black, gray, brown or yellow depending on the colour of the spores of the species in question. Fungi are capable of secreting certain enzymes with the help of which insoluble organic substances such as starch, cellulose, lignin and proteins are dissolved and absorbed. This ability of fungi makes them capable of thriving on a large variety of museum materials, under favourable environmental conditions.

Fungi are of different kinds and the term is a broad general designation used to refer to a heterogenous group of organisms including the many varieties of mushrooms. But most fungi are very small and several can be studied only with the aid of a microsope. The terms 'mould' and 'mildew' are applied to filamentous fungi whose growth on materials can usually be recognized by their fluffy or cottony appearance. The main part of the growth generally is white, but may also be coloured depending on the species. Tropical humid climates are the most favourable for the growth of fungi.

The damages brought about by fungi on objects range from simple chromatic alterations to serious weakening of the material. Fungus growth on museum objects have always been of great concern to Conservationists and has been the subject of considerable research by several workers in France, Italy, Japan and the United States. However, this field of research with particular reference to museum objects has not received adequate attention in India so far. Hence, a study of fungus attack on museum materials in India was undertaken by the author. The main purpose of the study was to identity the species that grow on various types of museum materials.

The morphology of fungi cannot satisfactorily be studied while they are on the objects affected. The host tissue may for example, be dark in colour making it difficult for microscopic examination, or sometimes isolation of the organism may not be rosy. More often than not, it is only the spores of the fungi that are seen on the object after the vegetative parts have withered out, making it rather difficult for a correct identification of the species. To overcome these problems the spores are to be isolated from the materials and cultures made in a suitable nutrient medium. The cultures are generally grown in Petri dishes containing a sterilized medium and stocks stored in test tubes on the same medium. Sterilization of the glassware and the medium are done by autoclaving.

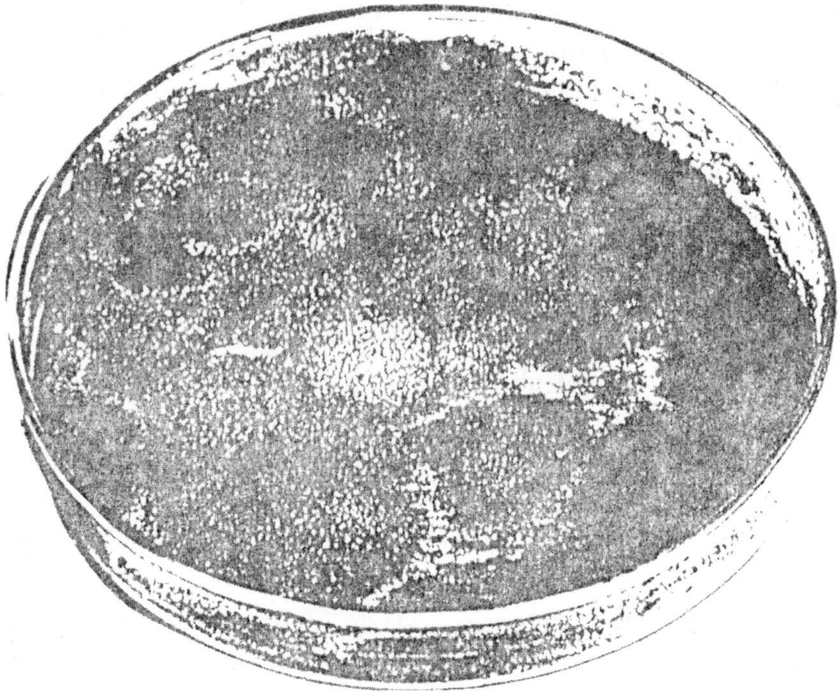

Fungus culture of spores isolated from a paper manuscript.

The Culture Medium

'Potato-Dextrose-Agar' medium (P.D.A.) was used for the culture in all the laboratory studies that were made. P.D.A. was prepared as follows: 20 gms. of peeled potatoes were sliced and boiled in about a litre of distilled water for about half an hour. The water was strained and 20 gms of Dextrose and Agar were dissolved in the remaining fluid. The liquid was then brought up to one litre by adding distilled water. The medium was then sterilized in an autoclave. Before P.D.A. is poured into the Petri dish 5 drops of 50% Lactic acid were added to it to avoid bacterial growth in the cultures.

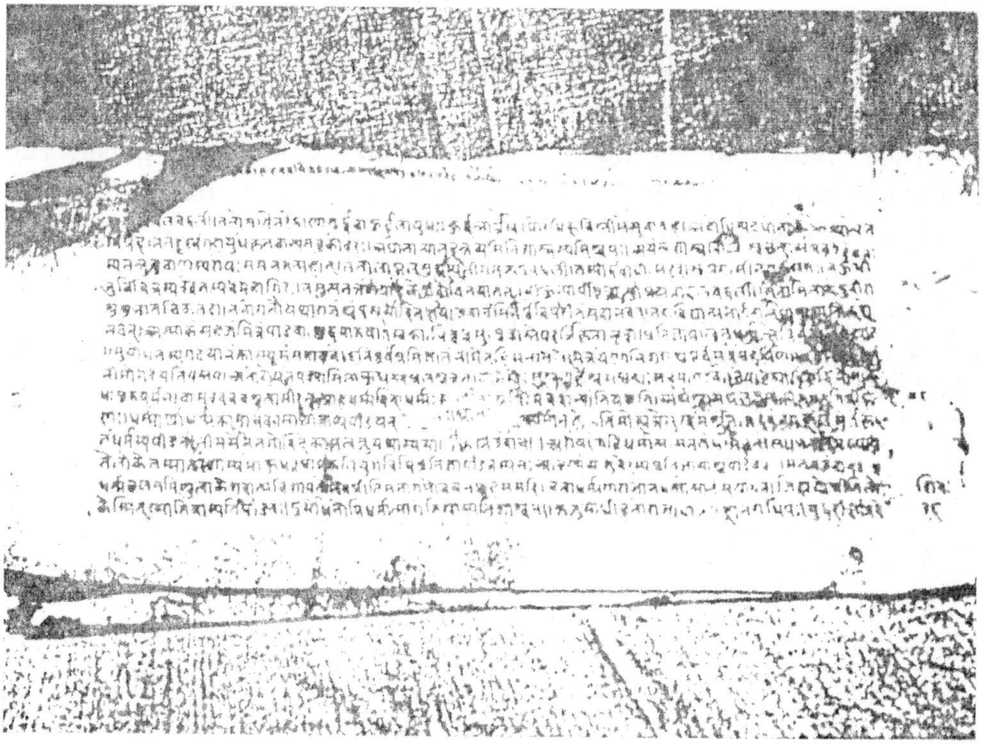

A paper manuscript showing black patches of fungal attack – Aspergillus niger.

Several species of fungi from various kinds of museum materials were isolated and the characteristics of some of the most common ones found are described below:

Aspergillus

Aspergillus is a widespread group of fungi. The distinguishing characteristics of this genus are as follows: Mycelium is septate and branched, usually colourless; the conidiophores are septate or non-septate and arising from a special mycelial cell which becomes enlarged and thick-walled. The conidiophore swells into a vescicle at the end which is elliptical, hemispherical or globose, bearing sterigmata from which the conidia originate. Conidia are in chains – generally green, brown or dark depending upon the species.

Aspergillus niger is found as black smooth colonies on paper. The conidiophores are colourless, but the conidial head is blackish brown or carbonous black. Distribution: more or less cosmopolitan, but more predominant in tropical humid regions. Highly celluloytic in character. *Aspergillus niger* was found to be more predominant then other fungi in some of the manuscripts examined. Other species of Aspergillus found were in bluish green colonies and *A. flavus* with colonies which appear green in colour.

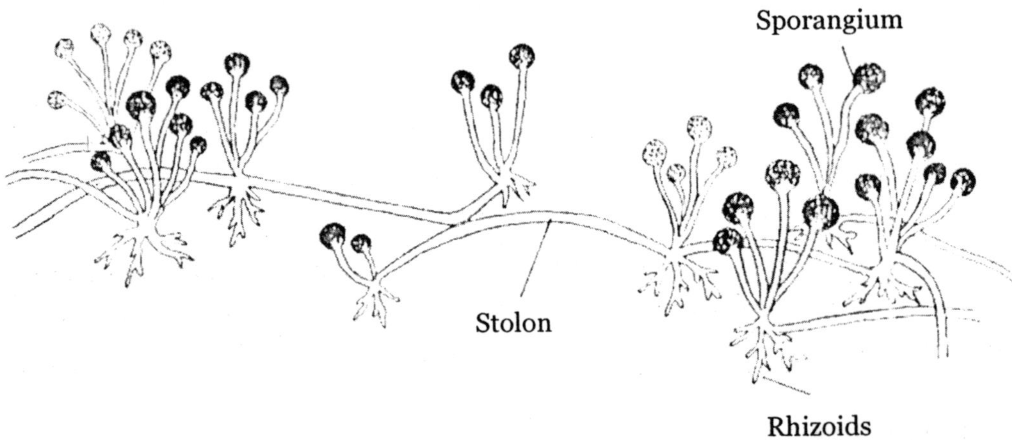

Structure of a typical mould fungus.

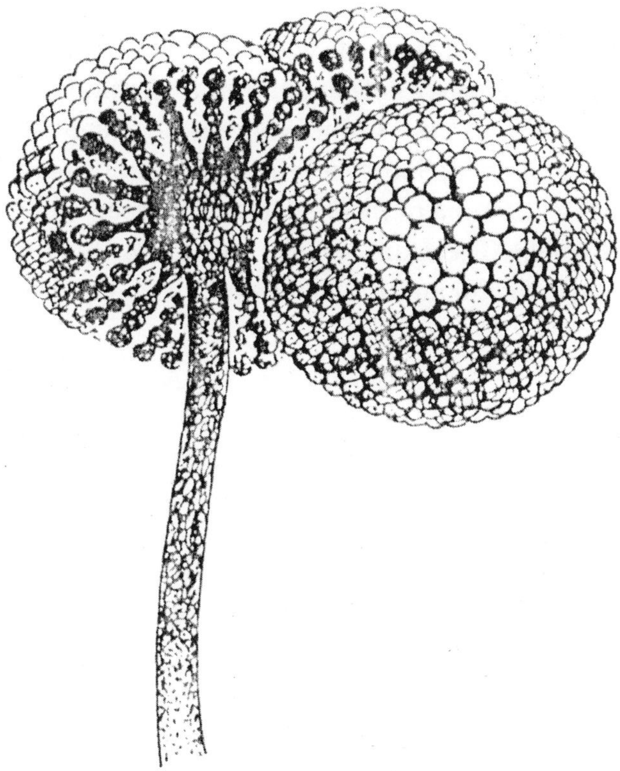

Conidia of Aspergillus niger.

ALTERNARIA

The genus *Alternaria* consists of fungi which have sterile, creeping hyphae that are mostly unbranched and short. Conidia are inverted club shaped, mostly elongate at the tip, dark coloured and lighter at the tip points, borne in more or less long, usually simple chains. The colour of the vegetative growth is dirty grey-green. The common Indian species of *Alternaria* are *A. humicola* and *A. malvae.*

PENICILLIUM

This is another fungus of widespread occurrence in India. The distinguishing characteristics of *Penicillium* are septate, branching mycelium that is usually colourless; Conidiophores are septate, perpendicular, branched or unbranched; Spore-bearing heads are brush-like with stigmata borne in clusters. Conidia of most species are green when young, but later may turn brownish. There are several species of this fungus including *P. rubrum, P. funicolosum* and *P. Chrysogenum* that are found on paper.

CURVULARIA

In the genus *Curvularia,* the mycellium are branched, septate, and brown in colour. Conidiophores are simple, thread-like, unbranched, septate and brown; thickly covered with conidia which are brown in colour, elipsoid or cylindrical in shapes, three or four septate, one of the central cells being distinctly larger and darker than the terminal cells. The common Indian species are *C. tetramera, C. maculans, and C. pallescens.*

TRICHODERMA

The mature mould of *Trichoderma* is bright green in colour. Mycelium and conidiophores are septate and many branched, the final branch being a sterigma, bearing terminally the conidial heads. Conidia are small and bright coloured. *T. album, T. lignorum* and *T. glaucum* are common Indian species of this group.

FUSARIUM

These fungi are generally yellow, purple or pink coloured. Conidial layer is cushion shaped or somewhat extended or arched; conidiophores branched; conidia terminal, simple, spindle shaped and many celled with distinct cross walls. There are several species of *Fusarium* in India including *F. clamydosporum* and *F. moniliformae*.

CLADOSPORIUM

The mycelium in *Cladosporium* is septate and dark; conidiophores are almost erect, branched and floccose, often forming a turf, olive gray to green in colour. Conidia are globose and obvate and dark, usually one-celled when young and may be two-celled when old. *Cladosporium herbarum* is a very common Indian species found growing on paper. They are seen in dark green colonies with blue green undersides and with dark mycelium and conidiophores.

LICHEN, LIVERWORT & MOSS

Plants like lichens, liverworts and mosses are often noticed on monuments and buildings. Lichen represents a symbiotic association between an alga and a fungus. The fungus is dependent on the alga for its food. The alga, with the help of sunlight, synthesizes food which is also provided for the fungus. The fungus absorbs and retains moisture that is utilized by the alga. Lichens are specially adapted to grow on rock surfaces. Liverworts and mosses prefer comparatively more moist surfaces. The liverworts derive their popular name from the fact that their thalli have a superficial resemblance to liver with its lobes. *Marchantia* and *Riccia* are the most common forms of liverworts. Moss plants grow on damp walls and similar situations during the rainy season. They grow in large tufts consisting of minute plants occurring in dense crowds. The upper part of the stem bears a cluster of bright green 'leaves'.

All three of the above plants grow on stone surface during favourable environmental conditions. Where as liverworts and mosses bring about comparatively minor deterioration on stone surface, lichens are known to disintegrate stone to a larger extent. Patchy discolorations and eventual loss of surface layer of stone are the result of lichen growth. All the three produce humic acid during their growth which is harmful depending upon the kind of stone.

INSECT PESTS

In countries which have a tropical or sub-tropical climate, special precautions against insect pests must be taken to safe-guard museum collections. A large variety of insects specially adapted for living, feeding and multiplying in museums are already known and reported from many countries. The literature search in the course of preparing this book brought to light hundreds of useful references. The problem of insects damaging the material belongings of man must be as old as man himself. Insects have been in existence for millions of years before man appeared on the earth. The earliest record of human concern with insect damage to materials goes back to the 3rd century B.C., when Aristotle, in his *Historia animalium* described damage caused to garments by certain insects. Evidence exists of the Chinese developing certain insecticides to protect paper, almost in the same period. In India there have been age-old methods of preserving materials using various 'home remedies'. These and other traditional pest control practices are reviewed in chapter V while dealing with control measures.

An account of the most common insect pests in museums, their characteristics, feeding habits and clues to identification are given below.

SILVER FISH (Lepisma Saccharina L.)

Silver fish is one of the most primitive insects belonging to the order, Thysanura. They are usually seen when books, papers, clothing or similar materials not in regular use are suddenly removed. When exposed to light, these fast moving insects glide quickly out of sight. They shun light and live in concealment. Museums, archives and libraries are therefore ideal places for them. They are also found in homes. Silver fish are one of the most injurious pests of libraries all over the world.

Silver fish has a distinct form, designated as "thysanuriform", meaning long and slender, broad at the fore-end, and tapering gradually to the rear. They are wingless and the body is covered with scales. Their metamorphosis is fairly simple, since the young look exactly like the adults, except that they are small in size.

The size of a silver fish ranges from 8 to 12. m.m. Their antennae, cerci and caudal filaments are as long as the body. The body tapers very markedly from head to tail and is covered with thin scales which give it a silvery shiny appearance. It has two long antennae which are many segmented and three similar appendages at the tail end. The mouth parts are adapted for biting. The female lays ten to fifty eggs which under favourable conditions hatch within 6 to 10 days. There is no larval stage in the case of silver fish as in other insects like beetles, moths etc. The nymphal stage (small young stage) lasts from three months to two years depending upon temperature and humidity. Temperature varying from 25 to 35°C and humidity above 55% are ideal conditions for their development. Under such conditions there may be three generations in one year.

Characteristic Damage

Silver fishes are mostly surface feeders. They show a particular affinity to flour glue, photographic gelatine, sizes and other glues. Irregular patches are found on the surface of book-bindings, papers, cards etc. eaten away by silver fish. They frequently eat off gold lettering on book covers to get at the paste beneath and also gnaw off label slips glued on the back of books, again because of the glue present. Silver fish can destroy heavily glazed paper, books and magazines printed on heavily sized paper, starched clothing, linens, lace or muslin, silks and rayons stiffened with sizing etc.

They also destroy wall papers and disfigure miniature paintings, prints and illustrated manuscripts.

BOOK LICE

Annoying, but usually harmless, these insects belonging to the order Psocoptera are tiny white or grayish white in colour, measuring in length between 1 and 1.5 m.m. (scarcely as long as the width of an ordinary pin head) They are found in abundance in damp, well shaded rooms not in general use such as store rooms. These little nuisances rarely damages books, paper or fabrics (silverfish and cockroaches are the real culprits). Psocids are of little importance as far as the biodeterioration of paper is concerned, except that their presence in large swarming numbers can be annoying. In one way it can be said that they even do a service to the book conservator by eating away the micro-fungi which develop on books during damp conditions of storage.

Book lice can be identified easily. They are called book lice because they are often seen on books and because they have some resemblance to the human head louse or the chicken louse. They are almost whitish when young, but as they grow older they become pale in colour. The body is more or less transluscent. Book lice can often be seen when opening old musty books. Their movement is peculiar, scurrying acros the pages in a halting and uncertain manner.

There are many species of book lice representing various families found throughout the world. The most common one found in India belongs to the family Liposcelidae, namely *Liposcelis divinatorius*. These are wingless forms. Other families of book lice are Phyllipsocidae, and Trogidae. *Trogium pulsatorium* L. is found in Europe and North America. *Liposcelis entomophilus* E. has been recorded in museums and libraries in the Phillipines. Many other species of Liposcelis are found in Africa, Hong Kong and Hawaii. *Psocatropus microps,* described as the common species in New Guinea, is also found in Africa, Java and Formosa. Other species of book lice are *Psocatropus lachlani* R, *Psyllopsocus minutissimus* E and *Ectopsocus maindroni* B reported from Hong Kong. In Sri Lanka there is a species of book lice, *Archipsocus fernandi*. Species of *Nepticulomina*, *Micropsocus* and *Tropusia are described* as book lice in Indonesia (Szent-Ivany, 19698).

Characteristic Damage

Psocids feed upon decaying timber, straw, feathers etc. In India large swarms of book lice can be noticed on the walls near flour mills, feeding upon the fine deposits of starchy flour. They do have an affinity for undried photographic gelatine and water colour paints. Artists who leave their water colour work with a fresh coat of colour in the evening may find the next day that irregular etchings are brought about by the feeding activity of these insects which have been active in the dark.

Psocids are not ordinarity considered as serious museum pests. In any case, the designation, 'book-lice' given to these insects is an injustice to them as they hardly do any damage to books. Though minute in size, book lice have relatively large heads and strong toothed mandibles. They damage dried entomological collections by devouring the scales and hairs on the bodies of insects, when storage boxes are not properly disinfected. They are known to damage herbarium collections also, particularly by eating away the pollen from dried flowers. Psocids prefer damp, warm undisturbed situations.

COCKROACHES

There is perhaps no habitable place in the world without cockroaches. There are about 3500 species of them, mostly found in the tropics. They are almost ommivorous and can cause damage to a variety of organic substances including food stuffs. Wool, leather, books, textiles etc. are susceptible to attack. They are also scavengers eating on organic filth of all kinds including dead insects. They are very much attracted to gums and glues and can be found occasionally drowned in gum bottles.

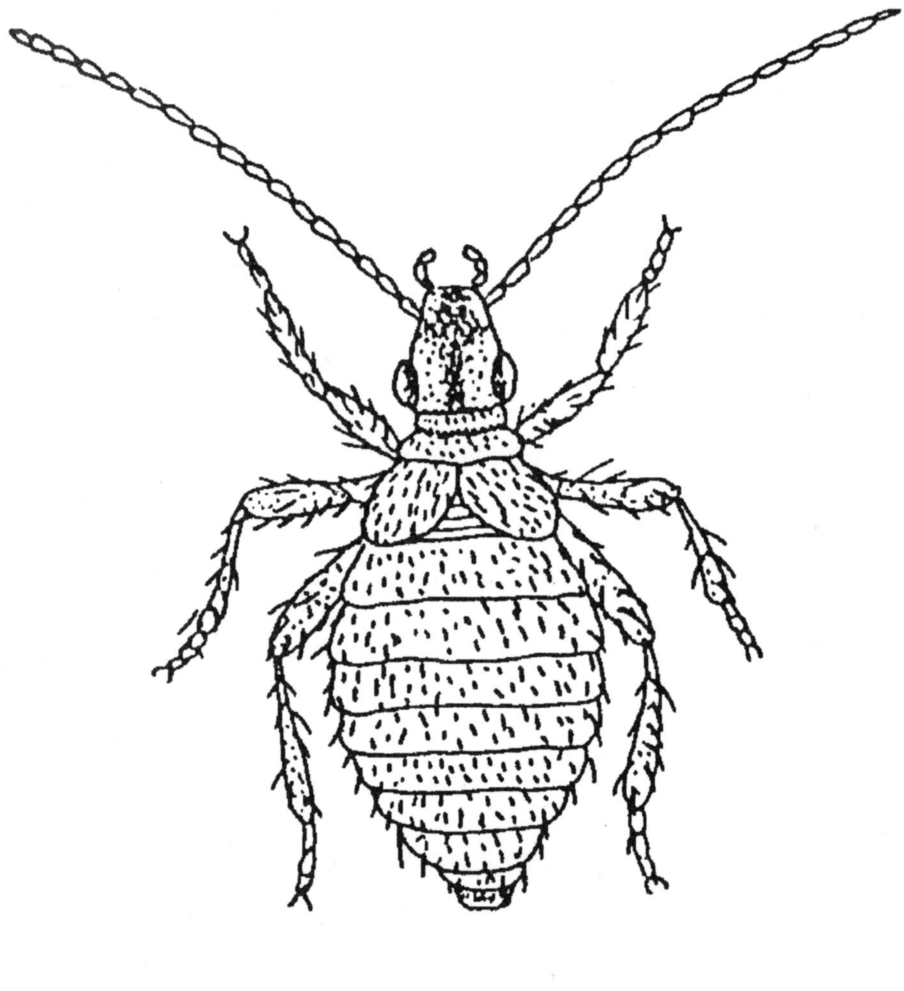

Book-louse, *Trogium pulsatorium* Adult.

Cockroaches are a highly successful species of the animal kingdom. Evolved in the early Silurian period, they have outlived many others and are abundant today with a cosmopolitan distribution. Their flattened bodies allow them to hide in small crevices, corners and gaps. They are nocturnal in habit. As soon as it is dark they come out of their hiding places. Cockroaches generally enter buildings through lavatories, drain pipes etc.

It is easy to identify cockroaches in general though one may not be able to distinguish the species. Most have wings, though there are a few without. The common species are the Oriental Cockroach (*Blatta orientalis L.*), the American Cockroach (*Periplanata Americana L.*), they German Cockroach (*Blattilla germanica L.*) the Australian Cockroach (*Periplanata Australasia*), the Brown Cockroach (*Periplanata Brunna B.*), and the Brown-banded Cockroach (*Supella supellectilium S.*).

HOUSE CRICKET

House crickets are jumping insects, closely related to the grass hoppers, belonging to the insect order Orthoptera. The common house cricket found in Indian is *Acheta domesticus* and it can be very destructive to paper, soft plant material, and they can feed on almost any kind of organic matter including other insects and carrion. The word 'cricket' is derived from the French word, "cricri", indicative of the cricket's chirping sound.

As with grass hoppers, the hind legs of crickets are modified for jumping. The adults are usually 2cm. long and pale-grey-brown with a black pattern on the head and thorax. They have two pairs of wings, of which the back pair is used for flying. They have strong biting mouthparts.

The House Crickets are usually nocturnal in habit. During the day they remain in wastepaper baskets and garbage dumps as well in undisturbed nooks and corners of buildings, behind book cases, wall hangings, framed photos etc. They become active during the night.

The species, *Acheta domesticus* is found in India and Europe. *Amphiacusta caraibea* Sauss is reported as a destructive pest to books and paper from Lesser Antilles. Another species, tropical in distribution, *Grylla crididae,* called 'tree crickets' is reported from New Guinea as a pest entering houses, attracted by electric light. It is known to cause cuts of various lengths in cloths, curtains, fabrics and sometimes paper. Yet another species, *Paragryllacris combustae* Germ. has been found to damage curtains in Australia. It is believed that this species cuts a piece from the material to form a flap under which it hides (Mc Keown, 1944 as quoted by Szent Ivani 1968).

WHITE ANTS (TERMITES)

White ants or termites are the most destructive pests of wood, particularly in the tropics. They may have existed in their present distribution for millions of years. The tropical species of termites belong to two main groups, namely, Sub-terranian termites and Dry-wood termites. The Sub-terranian species or ground nesting termites are by far more destructive to wood. Termites, though have many similarities to ants, belong to the insect order Isoptera, representing more than 2000 different species which are very different from ants. (Ants belong to the order Hymenoptera) Ants have thin waist lines whereas termites have thick waist lines.

Subterranian Ternites are social insects and they live in nests or colonies in the ground. The members of these colonies move in passageways that are hidden from the sun's rays and protected from undue moisture loss. Another instinct which is basic in the social habit of these insects is their ceaseless industry. They have never been observed to rest for any considerable length of time except while moulting. The colony consists of reproductive males and females, workers and soldiers. The worker is the one that destroys the wood and usually seen while examining termite affected wood. The soldiers are responsible for guarding the colony. the reproductives or sexual adults have yellow brown to black bodies with whitish transluscent wings, referred to as kings and queens. The termite queen is several times larger than other individuals in the colony. She develops a large abdomen which grows up to 130 mm. in certain species.

The damage caused to wood by termites is often not noticeable on the surface. They usually avoid exposure to air by constructing galleries within wood, leaving a thin outer shell. They do not reduce the wood to powder nor do they push out any powdery mass as the wood boring insects do. They construct flattened earthen tubes as passage ways between soil and wood which can be noticed on the walls of termite infested buildings. Apart from wood, termites also damage paper, boards, textile and fibres from plant sources such as cotton, jute, linen, coir etc. One may even come across non-cellulosic materials like plastics penetrated through and damaged by termites though they do not serve as food for them.

Subterranian termites are most abundant in moist, warm soil containing sources of food in the form of wood and other cellulosic materials. Such conditions are obtainable near buildings. In buildings where wood is used close to the ground infestation becomes easy. The main diet of termites is cellulose, which together with lignin make up the wood substance. They are unable to digest wood directly. Certain protozoa are present in the intestines of termites in large numbers, which break down the complex cellulose into sugars and thus making it available for termites. The moisture and temperature conditions necessary for the activities of termites are such that they also favour the development of wood inhabiting fungi. Furthermore, the termite galleries provide avenues for the rapid spread of fungus mycelium and thus the deterioration of wood is further aggravated. Termites are generally more harmful to buildings, structures and furniture than to objects in a museum.

The common species of termites found in South Asia, Thailand, Malayasia, Indo-China, Indonesia, Phillipines and Taiwan are listed by Roonwal (1979). 85 species of wood destroying sub-terranian termites are reported to be found in India. Some of these are *Odonotermes macrodentatus*, *Heterotermes indicola* (Wasmann), *Heterotermes gertrudae* Roonwal, *Macrotermes obesi* Holmgren, *Leucotermes indicola* and *Termes brunneus*.

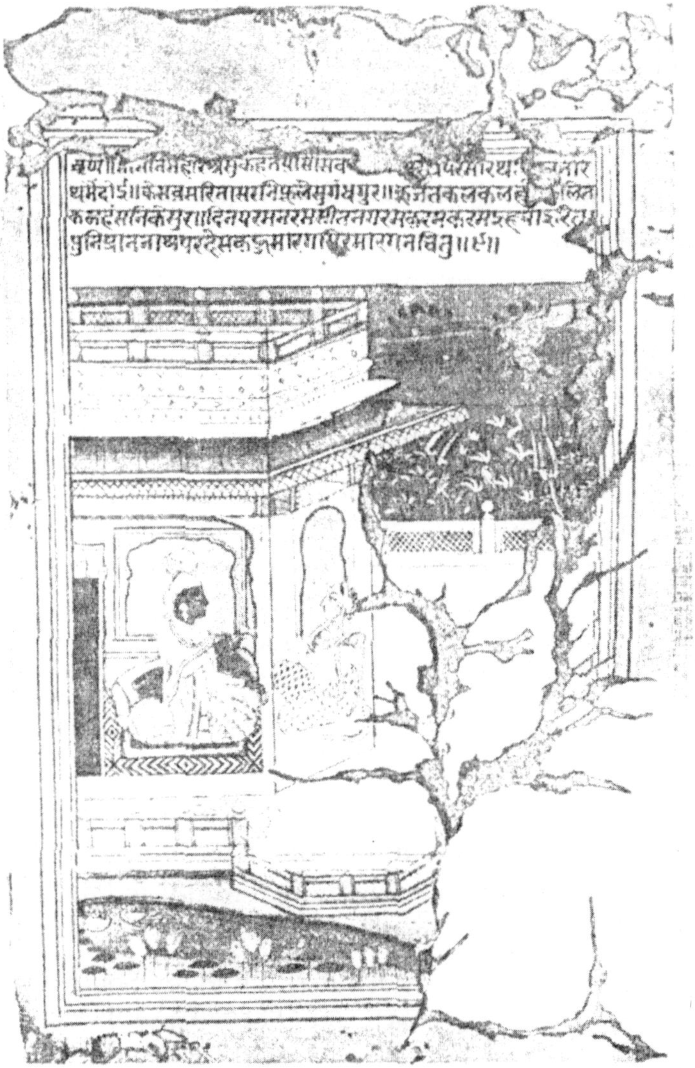

A Miniature painting attacked by sub-terranian termites.

Dry-wood termites also attack wood. They are called so because they establish themselves in wood that is not decayed and not in contact with ground. They are larger in size than sub-terranean termites. Dry wood termites in India include *Kalotermes jepsoni* Kemmer, *Neotermes buxensis* Roonwal and Sen Sharma and several species of the general. *Postelectrotermes, Kalotermes, Neotermes, Glyptotermes, Cryptotermes* etc.

For more information on termite species occurring in tropical South Asia the reader may refer to Roonwal's book on 'Termite life and Termite control in tropical South Asia', (1979).

WOOD-BORING BEETLES

Next to termites, the greatest damage to wood is caused by wood-boring beetles belonging to the insect order, Coleoptera. There are a large number of beetles, the grubs of which burrow into solid wood, often reducing it to a crumbling mass. The first sign of wood-borer infestation is the presence of small holes on the surface of the wood. Among the various wood-boring beetles the most injurious to wood in museums are those belonging to the families Anobidae (Furniture Beetle and Death-watch Beetle) and Lyctidae (Powder-post Beetle). A brief description of these insects is given below.

THE FURNITURE BETTLE

The Furniture Beetle, *Anobium punctatum* De Geer is the most common wood-boring insect and is found in many parts of the world. Infestations of this beelte are favoured by high humidity characteristic of tropical countries. The adult female lays up to 40 eggs in several groups in the cracks and crevices of wood. The eggs are white in colour and just visible to the naked eye. They hatch within three to four weeks and the larvae directly burrow into the wood. They can live on soft wood or hard wood as well as on sap wood and heart wood. The tunnels made by the larvae

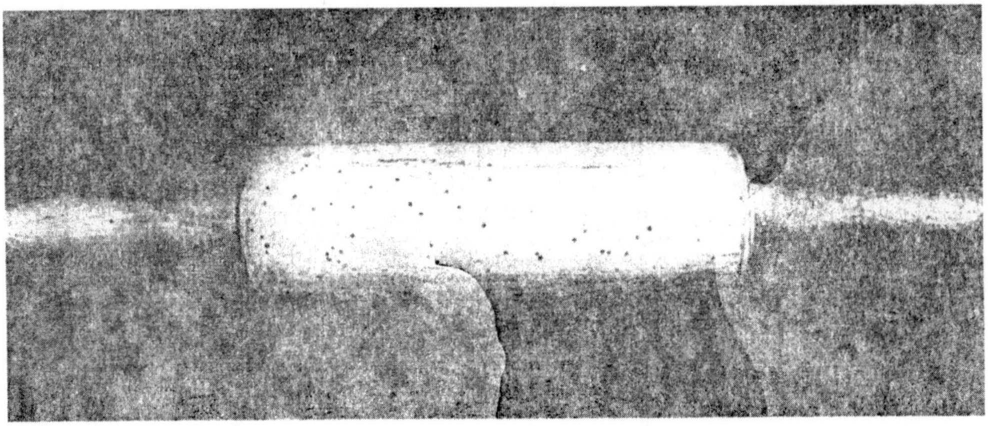

Exit holes of the Common Furniture Beetle, *Anobium punctatum* (Courtesy, Collin's Guie to Wild Life in House and Home)

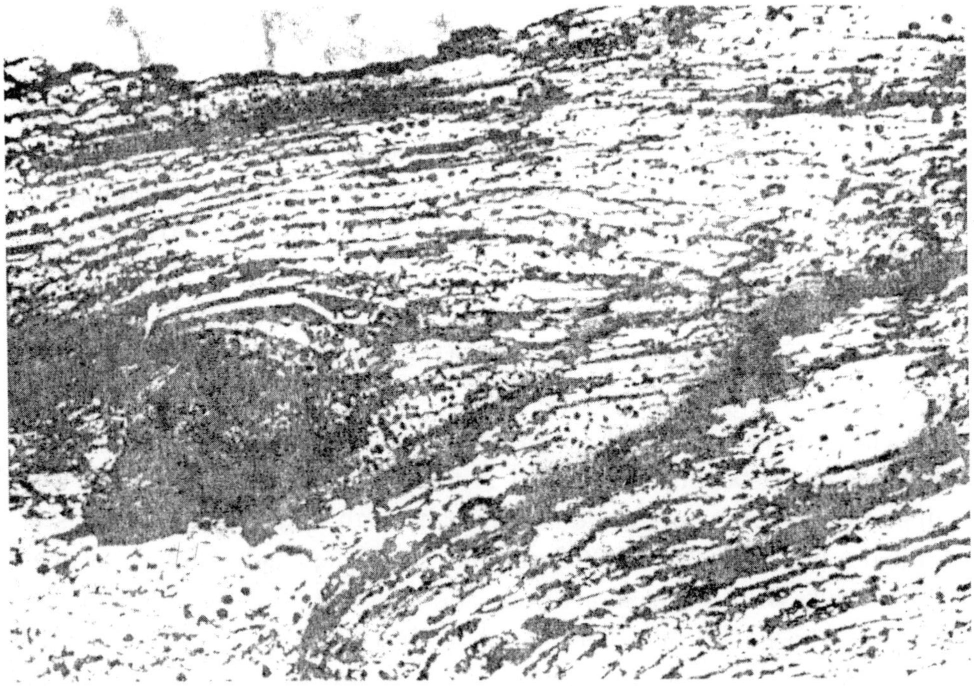

An oak beam damaged by Death-watch Beetle, *Xestobium rufovillosum.*

run more or less parallel to the grain structure and are packed with wood fragments and small spindle shaped faecal pellets. The larval life within the wood lasts from two to five years depending upon several factors.

The full grown larva is curved in appearance, almost 'C' shaped, with a wrinkled body having folds on which are seen rows of tiny dark brown hair like structures. The larva is white except for the head which is pale yellow with parts around the mouth reddish brown and the jaws nearly black. Just behind the head, on the lower side of the first three body segments are three pairs of short five-segmented legs. The hindmost body segments are somewhat longer and more swollen than those in front and are curved round so as to lie beneath them. The full grown larvae measure about 6.5 mm. in length.

When fully grown, the larvae tunnel towards the surface of the wood and excavate a slightly enlarged chamber, just below the outer layer of the wood to pupate. The pupal stage lasts between two and eight weeks depending upon temperature. On metamorphosis, the adult beetle bores to the surface of the wood and escapes. The exit holes are circular in shape, 1.5 to 3 m.m in diameter. The adults usually appear in warm summer months when the temperature and moisture conditions are favourbale. The beetles are reddish brown to dark brown in colour and vary in length between 2.5 and 5 mm. The dorsal side of the body is clothed with fine short yellow hairs and the wing covers are clearly marked with fine short yellow hairs with regular parallel longitudinal rows of pits. The pro-thorax forms a kind of hood to cover the head and bears long antennae and a circular eye on each side. The wings are fully developed and the beetles fly readily.

Apart from timber, the common furniture beetle is a serious pest of herbarium specimens and even books.

DEATH-WATCH BEETLE

Infestations of Death-watch Beetles, *Xestobium rufovillosum*, are often confused with that of the Furniture beetle. They can however be distinguished easily by the larger size of exit holes which are 2.5 mm to 4 mm. in diameter. The death-watch beetles are so called because they produce a tapping noise that is most often heard during the stillness of the night. Consequently the superstition developed that this tapping foretells that death is near because it was often heard by persons taking care of sick patients. In fact, the sound is made by the male insect striking its head or mandibles against the wooden walls which is believed to be a nuptial call to attract the females.

The adult female beetle lays about 200 eggs in crevices of the wood or in old exit holes. The white lemon shaped eggs hatch within two to eight weeks. The larvae are curved in shape and look very similar to those of the furniture beetle, but slightly larger in size. They often penetrate deeply into the heart wood and destroy the mechanical strength of the wood. Under normal conditions the life cycle lasts from four to five years in damp wood, but in dry wood it may last as long as ten years. The full grown larvae enter the pupal stage that lasts for a few weeks and the adult beetles come out by making holes in the wood.

Death-watch beetles can easily be distinguished from the furniture beetle by their larger size (6.5 to 9 mm. in length), darker, mottled colour and by the absence of regular longitudinal lines of pits one the wing covers. Infestations of these beetles are often of long standing nature and found in old buildings and wooden collections.

POEDER-POST BEETLE

Power-post beetles belong to the Coleopteran family of Lyctidae. They are one of the most serious pests of wooden objects and structural wood in museums all over the world. Though they have a preference for the sap wood portion of timber most of the hard woods are also prone to attack.

The biology of Lyctids has been studied by many entomologists. The female beetle lays about 30 to 60 eggs which are pushed into the surface pores and crevices of the wood by its long ovipositor. The eggs are long, oval or cylindrical and usually have a conical cap. Under favourable conditions they hatch out in 6 to 15 days. The larvae are 'C' shaped, white in colour, except for the head which is dark brown and the mandibles that are brownish black. The anterior end is relatively larger than the posterior end. One of the distinguishing features of Lyctus larvae, in comparison to the larvae of other wood boring insects is that the last pair of spiracles (8th pair) are much larger than the other spiracles. The larva has three pairs of three-jointed minute legs on the anterior portion of its body. The length of larval life varies from three to nine months. When fully grown, the larvae bore upwards and within a depth of 4 mm. from the surface of the wood make small cylindrical pupal chambers in which they pupate. The pupal stage lasts for about three to four weeks.

The adult beetles emerge by boring their way to the wood surface. The beetles are small, abut 6 mm. long and the body is elongate and somewhat flattened. They are brown to black in colour. The head is not covered by prothorax. The terminal part of the antennae is club shaped. The adult beetles have a pubescence on their wing covers, the arrangement of which helps to distinguish the species.

Wood severely and repeatedly attacked by powder-post beetles is nearly reduced to powder from inside, leaving the exterior shell intact. The extend of infestation is correlated with the amount of starch present in the wood. The infested wood can be detected by the presence of small piles of flour like frass on the floor surfaces below the wooden object or structure. The exit holes are circular and about 1 to 1.5 mm in diameter. The wood dust that falls out is extremely fine, almost like talcum powder, to touch.

These characteristics should help identify powder post-beetle infestation without any difficulty.

The most common powder-post beetle in India is *Lyctus brunneus*. It is found in many parts of the world. *Lyctus linearis* is reported to be common in Britain and Europe (Mourier and Winding, 1975). *Minthea rugicollis* W., another species is known to cause severe damage to ethnographic specimens such as masks and wood-carvings in Indonesia (Szent-Ivany, 1968). Lyctus attack has been noticed in wooden objects and structural timber including ply woods both inside and outside museums in several parts in India. *Lyctus panicollis* Lec. and the velvety Lyctus, *L. parallelepipedus* Melsh are reported from the United States of America. *Minthea migicollis* Walker, a tropical species is said to cause extensive damage to wood,particularly ply wood, sports goods and furniture in the Malay Peninsula.

THE BAMBOO-BORER

The Bamboo borer or the Bamboo powder-post beetle, *Dinoderus minutus* Fabricium, belonging to the family Bostrichidae is a cylindrical brown beetle, three to four mm. long and a native of Asia. It is a pest primarily of bamboo products. It breeds in bamboo, reducing the inner area into a fine power.

Eggs hatch in about three to seven days. The larval life is approximately 6 weeks and the pupal period about 4 to 5 days.

BOOK-WORM BEETLES

Book-worm infection of manuscripts, documents and books has been recorded by authors from many parts of the world. Most of these reports refer to serious damage caused to archival materials in tropical humid regions particularly India, Burma, Indonesia, Malaya and the Hawaii

Islands. It is interesting to note that the insects described as book-worms in different parts of the world are not always the same species. Some confusion appears to have existed as to the exact identity of the so called book-worms. Evans (1949) states that several species belonging to the generae *Catorama, Dorcatoma, Stegobium* and *Gastrullus* made up the book-worms. *Gastrallus laticollis* Pic. has been recorded by Kalshoven (1938) from Indonesia which was earlier reported from Hawaii by Swezey (1930). Among other book-worms recorded from Indonesia are *Lasioderma serricorne* and *Catoroma herbarium. Ptilinus testaceous* Pic. has been mentioned as harmful to books in Malaya (Pic. 1936). Back (1947) writes about the ravages caused by a species of book-worm beetle, *Neogastrallus librinoceous.* Fausta galla (1963) refers to another species of *Gastrallus,* namely, *G. immarginatus* are harmful to books.

The Indian Book-worm Beetle

The Indian Book-worm Beetle is identified as *Gastrallus indicus* Reitter (Order: Coleoptera; Family: Anobiidae) It has been recorded from many parts of India and Burma. Punjab, Dehra Dun, New Delhi Mandalay (Burma) etc. are all places where *Gastrallus* infection of paper have been recorded. Information is also available about their attach on old palm-leaf records in Trivandrum (Kerala). *Gastrallus indicus* infestation on books and palm leaf manuscripts has been observed by the author in many libraries and museums in India.

It is common experience to many that books and old manuiscripts which are so badly damaged, when examined, reveal not a single living book-worm. Most books are found badly burrowed by book-worms, but completely free from any living form. This is due to parasites and predators like *Attagenus, Anthrenus* etc. that are natural enemies of book-worms. Actually it is very rare that one can get living specimens of this insect to study. The author was successful in collecting gastrallus larvae from book-bindings from Hyderabad which facilitated continued laboratory culture and the study reported here.

The affected books were examined carefully to study the nature of damage caused by the larvae. The larval activity was found to be more predominant within the book-bindings, though this was not revealed by surface examination alone. The bindings were composed of card board made up of unbleached wood pulp with a thin leather layer pasted on the outer cover. The adhesives used seemed to be starch paste. The leather surface shoed a number of small round holes. Inside the binding, underneath the leather layer a large number of tunnels made by the larvae were visible. The larvae had made parallel sided tunnels of about 1 to 1.5 mm. wide running in all directions. These galleries were filled with irregular shaped faecal pellets. Occaionally the larvae must have also tunneled into the pages of the book as revealed by the galleries that run into the pages. This is because the eggs are laid near the surface of the book-bindings or on the edge of the leaves. The freshly hatched larvae eat their way into the interior of the book-binding and the book. Heavily infected book-bindings are riddled with a number of galleries inside but the surface cover shows only a few circular holes. The holes seen on the surface are the emergence holes through which the adult beetles come out after metamorphosis.

There is hardly any comprehensive account available about the morphology or life cycle of *Gastrallus indicus.* The only published references available about the insect are a paper by Mukerji (1954) dealing with the genitalia of the beetle and another by Roonwal and Chatterjee (1951) dealing with a method of heat treatment for the eradication of book-worms. The life history of *Gastrallus indicus* Reitter has not been studied by anyone hitherto.

With the larvae obtained from book-bindings it was possible to obtain the pupal and adult stages and to maintain a laboratory culture of the insect. It was observed that the larvae undergo natural feeding and development only when hidden inside the book-binding or the pages, and that when

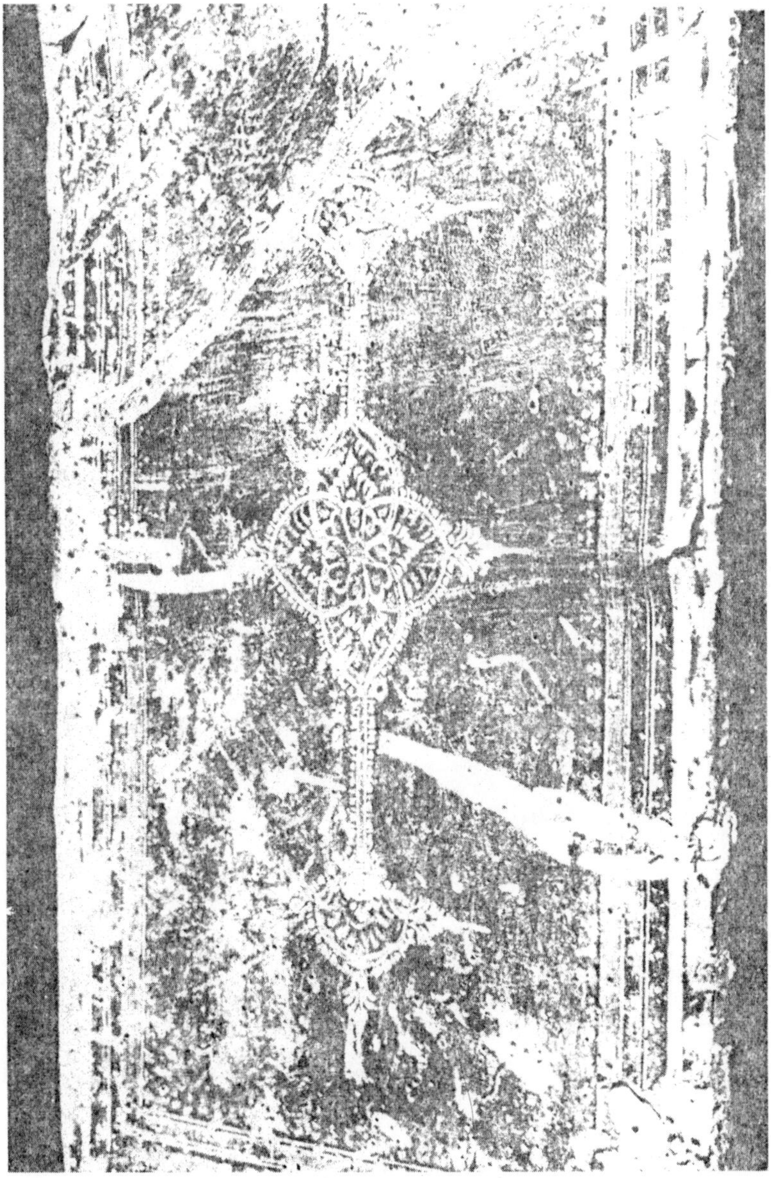

A book-binding attacked by the Indian Book-worm Beetle, *Gastrallus indicus*.

A book binding, part of the upper leather removed to show the larval galleries made by the Indian Book-worm Beetle, *Gastrallus*.

Leaves of a book showing attack by the Indian Book-worm Beetle, *Gastrallus indicus*.

exposed they remain inactive for several days after which they bore their way inside and disappear underneath. This habit of the larvae poses and obvious difficulty for studying the life history of the insect.

The Larva

The mature larva is about 3 to 4 mm. long and has a stout white semi-cylindrical and crescent shaped body with the thorax comparatively swollen, and it very much resembles the larva of the powder-post beetle. There are three pairs of tiny thoracic legs. The grubs that hatch from the eggs start burrowing into the book and show a definite preference for the binding, seemingly attracted by the glue, paste and the raw wood pulp that go into the composition of old book-bindings. Very often they centre their feeding activity along the backs or hinges of the book covers cutting the threads that bind the pages together, thus causing the pages to fall apart. From these original points of attack, the grubs as they become more mature and voracious, extend their tunnels through the cover and pages and line their tunnels and pupal chambers with a glue like secretion which makes the pages stick together. The excreta of the grubs gather in the larval galleries and between the pages as a fine dust that may be as varied in colour as the differences in the type of binding or paper ruined through their feeding. From badly damaged books, this powder or dust will sift out when the book is shaken and can sometimes be collected in large quantitities. The larval period ranges from three to six months depending upon temperature and humidity conditions. The pupal stage is usually between 7 to 14 days.

The Adult

The adult beetles, almost impossible to find without a close search are small, slender and testaceous brown in colour (paler and some-what ochraceous when immature). They measure about 2 to 3 mm. long and about 1 mm. wide. The body has smooth parallel sides. These beetles are inconspicuous and are seldom active in bright light. The adult beetle which matures close beneath the cover or the edge of the pages escape from the book by eating small round holes, usually about 1 mm. or less in diameter. The beetles must reach the exterior to mate and lay eggs.

The Indian Book-worm beetle is a serious pest of books, manuscripts and documents including palm leaf.

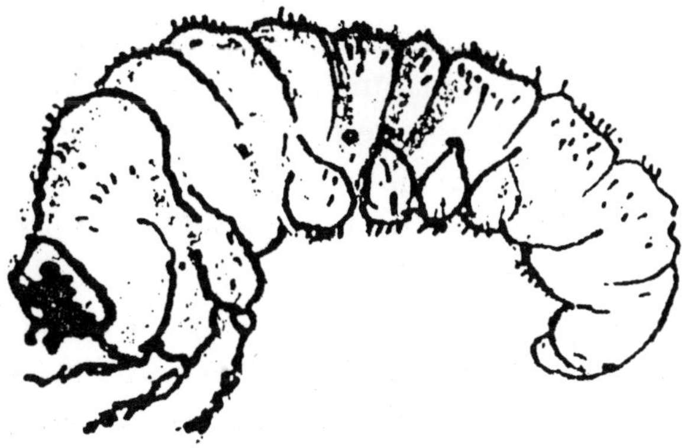

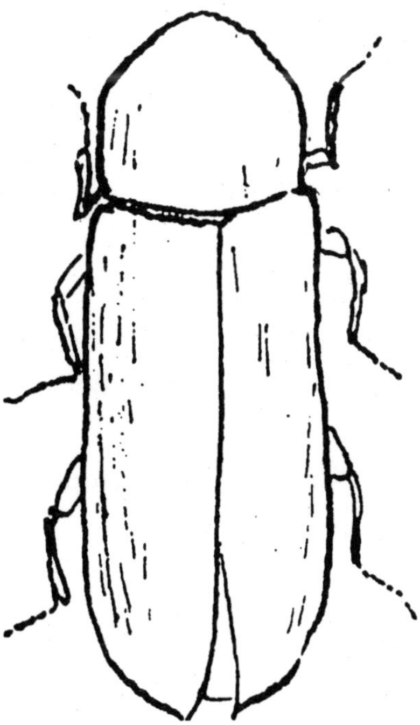

Larva and adult of the Indian Bookworm Beetle, *Gastrallus indicus*.

Dermestid Beetles

Of all the insects known to cause damage to materials, the dermestid beetles are the most harmful. About 52 species of *Dermestidae* are recorded as pests of stored products throughout the world (Patel, 1958).

The name *dermestidae* has originatedfrom a Greek word meaning, "to devour a skin". Dermestids are known to feed on a variety of materials of both animal and plant origin. These include skins, hides, leather, taxidermy specimens of birds and mammals, hair, fur, feather, carpets, woolen fabrics, entomological specimens, cereals and cereal products. It is believed that originally the larvae fed on hides, skins, wool, hooves, horns, feathers etc. of careasses found lying on the ground in the open. Artificial conditions created by man in households, stores, museums, libraries etc. have proved so ideal for the development of some species of dermestids that they have been drawn from their natural habitats adapting to a new mode of life. The adults of several species still live outdoors frequenting flowers and probably feeding on pollen (Hinton, 1945).

Today, dermestid beetles are distributed throughout the world, inhabiting a wide range of ecological niches and feeding on a variety of materials.

The general characheristics of Dermestid Beetles are as follows:

1. The dermestid beetles, as do all beetles, go through a complete metamorphosis. Life cycle: egg, larva, pupa & adult.
2. All adult beetles have a very compact, seed like appearance because legs, antennae and head fit snugly to the body. The head is comparatively small.
3. The larvae are extremely hairy, the entire body being completely covered with bristles or long hairs.
4. The larvae are comparatively very active.
5. Both adults and larvae frequently play possum when distrubed.

6. It is the general characteristic of the dermestids that the pupal stage is developed inside the last larval skin.
7. The larvae of dermestids in general can withstand considerable starvation.
8. Deterioration to materials is brought about by the larvae only.

The dermestids in general possess certain remarkable adaptations enabling them to live under varied nutritional and environmental conditions. They can thrive on a variety of organic materials without imbibing water, withstand fairly wide variations of temperature and humidity and survive long periods of starvation when food supply fails. The egg production is autogenous, the majority of eggs being laid without feeding, which again is a definite advantage for the survival of the species.

A large number of dermestid beetles, belonging to the genera *Anthrenus, Attagenus, Dermestes* and *Trogoderma* are recorded as pests in museums. According to Patel (1958), the genus *Anthrenus* alone accounts for & different major pest species. These are *Anthrenus flavipes* Le Conte (Furniture-Carpet Beetle), *Anthrenus scrophulariae* (Linnaeus)(Common Carpet Beetle), *Anthrenus verbasci (*Linnaeus) (Varied Carpet Beetle), *Anthrenus museorum* (Linnaeus) (Museum Beetle), *Anthrenus pimpinellae, Anthrenus Coloratus* Reit, *Anthrenus fuscus* Oliver and *Anthrenus caucasicus.*

The common museum pests of the genus *Attagenus* are *Attagenus gloriosae, Attagenus pellio* and *Attagenus elongates* all known as Carpet Beetles, *Attagenus megatoma* (Black Carpet Beetle) and *Attagenus fasciatus* (Wardrobe Beetle).

The genus *Dermestes* contain pest species such as *Dermetstes vulpinus* Fabricius (also named as *Dermestes maculates* De Geer) commonly known as the Hide Beetle or Leather Beetle, *Dermestes frischi* kug also known as Hide Beetle, *Dermestes lardarius* Linnaeus (Larder Beetle) and *Dermestes ater* De Geer (Black Larder Beetle).

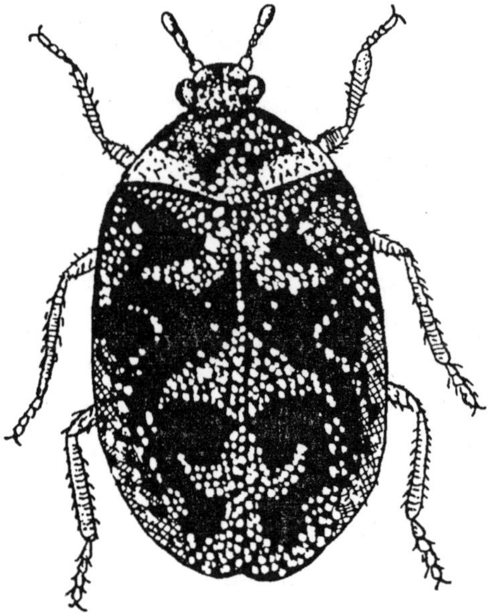

Museum Beetle, *Anthrenus museorum.*

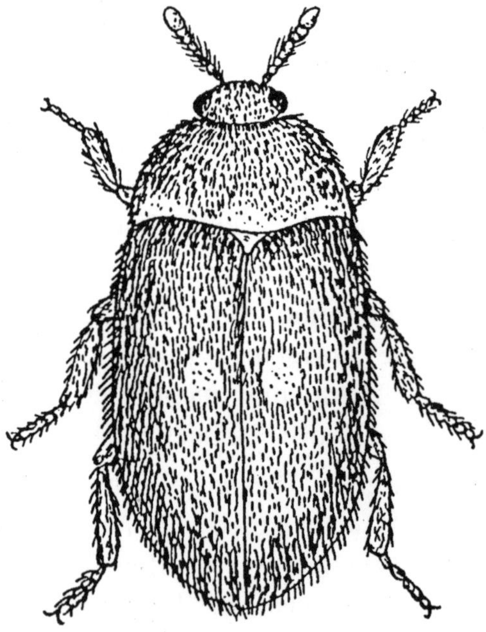

Carpet Beetle, *Attagenus pellio.*

The genus *Trogoderma* consists of *Trogoderma granarium* Everts (Khapra Beetle),Trogoderma ornatum (Say) (Cabinet Beetle) *Trogoderma variabile* Ballion (Warehouse Beetle) and *Trogoderma inclusum* Le Conte also known as Cabinet Beetle.

The Furniture Carpet beetle *Anthrenus flavipes* Le Conte is the most abundant and highly harmful species of the dermestids found in India. The survey of biodeterioration of museum materials undertaken in India by the author has shown that the major part of the damage caused to proteinaceous materials in museums is done by the larvae of this beetle. A detailed account of the biology and feeding habits of the Common dermestid beetles found as pests of museum materials in India is given below.

THE FURNITURE-CARPET BEETLE

The Furniture-carpet Beetle, *Anthrenus flavipes* Le Conte is the most widely distributed and the most harmful of the several species of dermestid beetles found in India. Considerable damage to natural history specimens, upholstered furniture and woolen fabrics caused by the larvae of *Anthrenus flavipes* has been reputed from many museums.

In India, *Anthrenus flavipes* was first recorded from Madras Presidency in 1883 by Waterhosue and later by Cotes (1890), found on dried mammalian skins in the Indian Museum, Calcutta. The larva of this beetle is particularly adapted for feeding on keratinous materials. It was observed that considerable feeding occurs on woolen garments and fabrics, carpets, dry-preserved entomological specimens, stuffed birds and mammals, horn and antler, fur, feather and hair among museum collections.

The eggs of *Anthrenus flavipes* are elongate, oval in shape and slightly broader at one end. The surface of the egg is somewhat wrinkled and there are a group of spine like projections at one end which serve to attach to the surface upon which it is deposited. The egg is iridescent white when freshly laid, but gradually changes to a pale yellow colour. In size they measure 0.6 mm to 0.9 mm in length and 0.25 mm to 0.4 mm in width. Just before hatching the head capsule and body hairs of the larva become visible through the egg shell.

Back and Cotton (1936) reported that the female beetle lays 37 to 96 eggs; Hocking (1943) states that the number of eggs laid ranges from 40 to 100; Sohi (1951) observed that 11 to 52 eggs were laid by the female; Patel (1958) states that the maximum eggs laid was 36, contradicting earlier authors. In the present study it was observed that 42 to 74 eggs per females was laid.

Temperatures between 30 to 32 degrees Centigrade are most ideally suited for the development of the egg of *Anthrenus flavipes* though they survive very well in higher ranges of temperature of even upto 40°C. Humidity, does not have any appreciable variation in the incubation period. It should be pointed out that the temperature range mentioned above is usually obtainable within museums throughout India for most parts of the year.

The Larva

The newly hatched larva has creamy white colour, with an elongate oval body, densely clothed with dark hair. The duration of the larval stage is also markedly influenced by temperature and the nature of food taken. The larvae start feeding soon after emergence. The full grown larvae vary considerably in size. The larva, on average, measures about 5 mm in length and 2 mm. in width and weighs about 6 mgs. The body has a thick coat of easily detachable hairs which has earned for it the popular name "wooly bear".

Experiments aimed at finding out the most suitable of museum materials that would sustain a complete development of the adult and would repeat generations were conducted. Larvae, 10 days old were introduced in several food materials and observed for 60 days at temperature 31 ±

1 degree Centigrade and an approximate relative humidity of 70%. The following table shows the number of larvae which were able to complete development and initiate a new generation on the various materials.

Food material	*No. of larvae introduced*	*No. of adults emerged*
Dried insects	20	16
Horn	-	17
Feather	-	16
Hair,Fur	-	16
Wool	-	19
Incompletely cleaned skeleton	-	5
Sponge	-	All died
Leather (Chrome tanned)	-	-
Dried Star fish	-	-
Dried Crab	-	-

These observations show that the materials that readily sustain the growth and development of the larvae are wool, horn, feather, dried insects, hair and fur. Chrome tanned leather did not sustain the growth of the larvae, probably due to the presence of chromic oxide.

The Pupa

When the larva is full grown, a split is formed on the dorsal side of the skin and the pupa remains enclosed in it during the pupal stage. The pupa is creamy white in colour, but it can be distinguished from the larva only on close observation because it is the last larval skin that encloses the pupa.

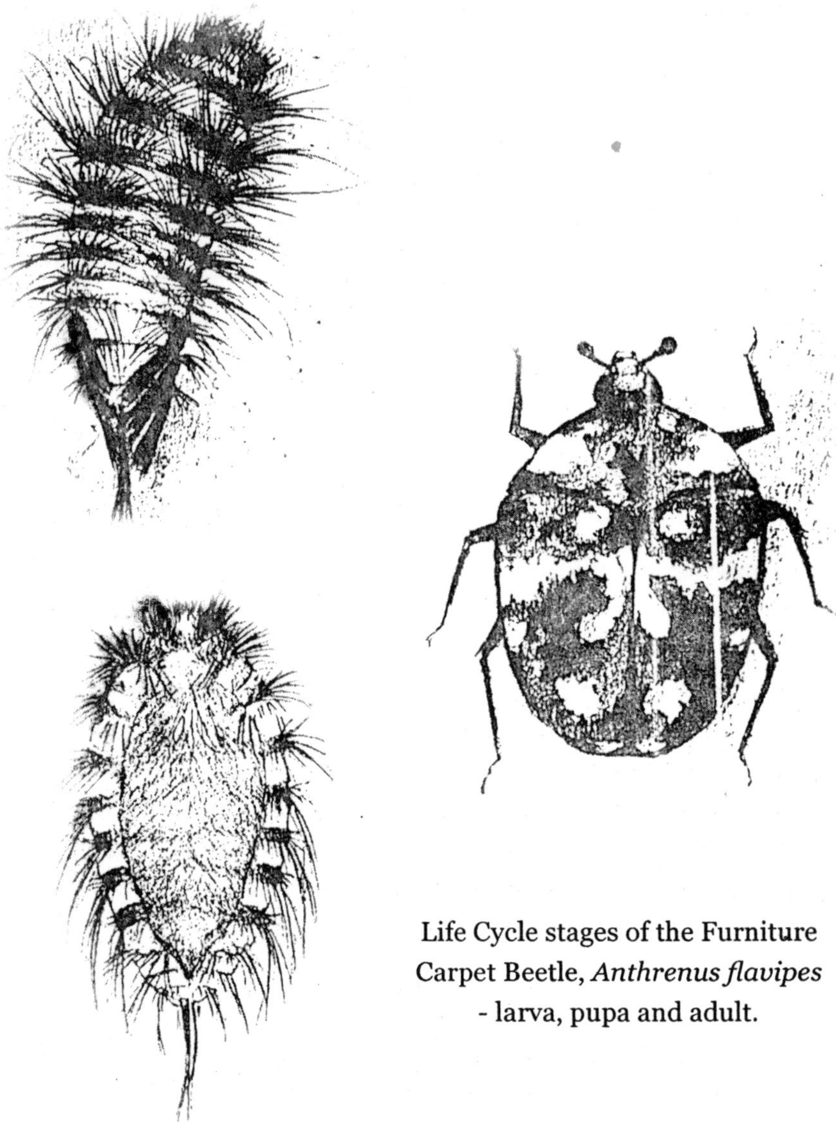

Life Cycle stages of the Furniture Carpet Beetle, *Anthrenus flavipes* - larva, pupa and adult.

Temperature between 30 and 35 degrees Centigrade are favourable for the metamorphosis of the insect from the pupal stage to the adult.

The fully formed adult comes out of the pupal skin and remains within the last larval skin in which it pupated, for a couple of days to even a week. This is known as the pre-emergent or quiescent adult stage. Afterwards, the adult comes out of the larval skin and becomes active.

The Adult

The adult beetle measures about 3.5 mm. in length and 2.5 mm. in breadth. The body is covered with glistening white, imbricate scales on the ventral surface and by coloured scales – black, yellowish brown and white arranged in definite patches so as to form a mottled pattern on the elytra, thorax and head. The adult, though found non-feeding under laboratory conditions, possesses the usual coleopteran type of mouth parts.

Ayyappa *et. al.* (1957) observe that temperature has a marked effect on the duration of the adult stage. According to them the adults lived longer at 25 degrees Centigrade than at 30 degrees Centigrade and above. In the present studies in was observed that adults live approximately for one month at 30 degrees centigrade.

THE HIDE (LEATHER) BEETLE

Dermestes vulpinus Farbrius (*maculates* De Geer), belonging to the same order and family as that of the Furniture Carpet Beetle, is popularly known as the Leather Beetle or Hide Beetle. It is also a cosmopolitan species, the larvae of which feed on dead animal matter, hides and skins, taxidermy specimens, leather and leather goods. The full grown larvae of this beetle have the peculiar habit of leaving the food supply to find a suitable place for pupation. They bore their pupal chambers in almost any compact substance that happens to be near at hand. This habit of indiscriminate boring into materials which they do not use as food has frequently been noted. According to Hinton (1945) the larvae have been known to bore into cork, fibre board, books, stored tobacco including cigarettes and cigars, linen, cotton, wool, salt, sal ammoniac, plaster moulds, flexible asbestos, and even lead. A considerable part of the economic loss due to this species is attributed to this habit of the mature larvae.

In India, the larvae of *Dermestes vulpinus* were found feeding upon museum specimens of birds, mammals, hair, feather, fur, dried entomological collections, wool, bristles of brushes, horn, antler etc. Feeding response studies show that the larvae have a strong preference for leather, raw hides and skins as well as dried fish. The insects for the present studies were obtained from a natural infestation in some poorly preserved study skins of birds.

The egg is cylindrical in shape, slightly broader at one end and about thrice as long as broad, usually measuring about 1.6 mm long and 0.5 mm broad. The egg, when freshly laid was observed to be creamy white in colour, but gradually changes to brown. Incubation period of the egg is about 2 to 3 days at 28 to 30 degrees centigrade. Humidity dit not show any appreciable effect on the incubation period. At temperatures above 40 degrees centigrade the eggs failed to hatch.

The Larva

The newly hatched larva is creamy white in colour with light brown bands on the dorsal surface and is densely clothed with dark brown or black hairs. The larva is elongate and tapering at the posterior end. They are active & negatively phototropic in behaviour. The freshly hatched larva is about 2 mm. long and 0.5 mm broad whereas the full grown larva measures about 10 mm. in length and 2 mm. in breadth.

The larvae are voracious feeders and the maximum damage to materials is caused in the larval stage. They moult a variable number of

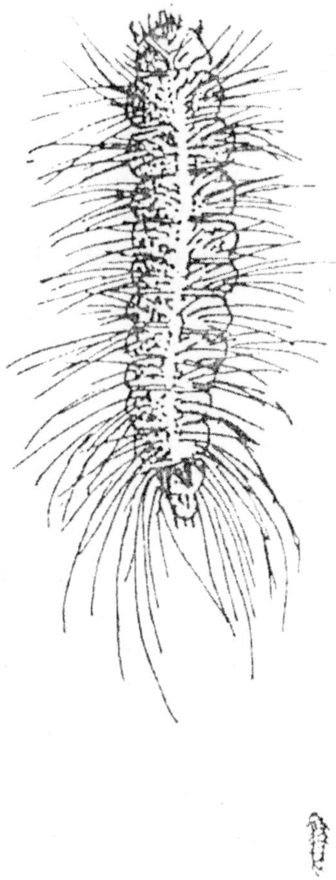

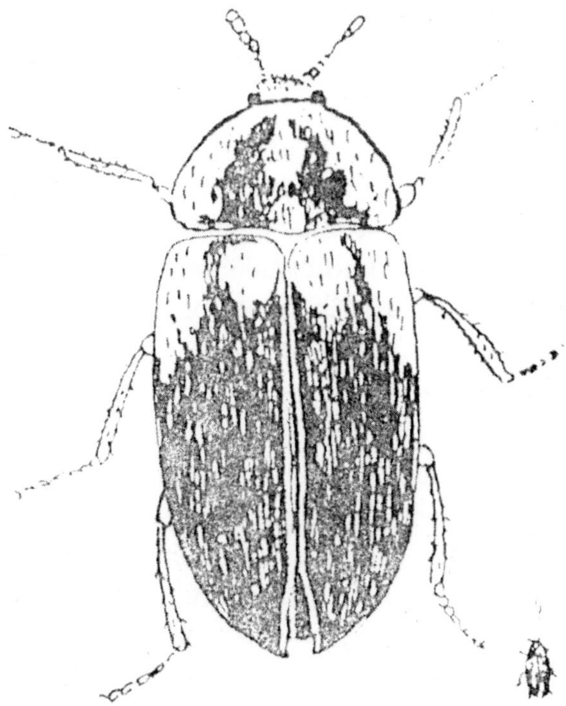

Larva and adult of
the Leather Beetle,
Dermestes vulpinus.

times (7 to 14) before reaching maturity. The larval development was found to depend upon temperature, humidity and the amount and kind of food available.

Experimental studies showed that only at high humidities with temperatures ranging between 25 and 30 degrees centigrade was the development of the larvae at its best. Between 28 and 30 degrees centigrade and with 90% rH the larvae developed in the shortest period of 25-30 days. They failed to develop at 40 degrees centigrade and above.

The Pupa

Pupation usually takes place in the last larval skin. At the end of the larval period the skin of the larva splits on its dorsal side. The split starts from the anterior end and proceeds up to the middle of the back and the pupa is formed. The average size of the pupa is about 7 mm. long and 2.7 mm. wide. Temperature had an appreciable effect on the pupal period whereas humidity had no influence, other than a slight reduction of the pupal period, mostly less than half-a-day.

Between 28 and 30 degrees centigrade the pupae take the minimum number of days for emergence. It was also observed that during the cold winter months they take as many as 35 to 40 days for emergence. The pupae failed to complete development at 40 degree centigrade and above.

The Adult

The adult emerges at the end of the pupal period, casting off the larval skin in which it has pupated and starts actively moving about. It measures about 6.5 mm. to 9 mm in length and 3 mm. to 4 mm. in width. The body is sub-parallel in shape and the cuticle usually shining black in colour. The dorsal surface is densely clothed with hair. The adult is a fast runner and tries to hide at the slightest disturbance. The beetle usually lives for 7 to 20

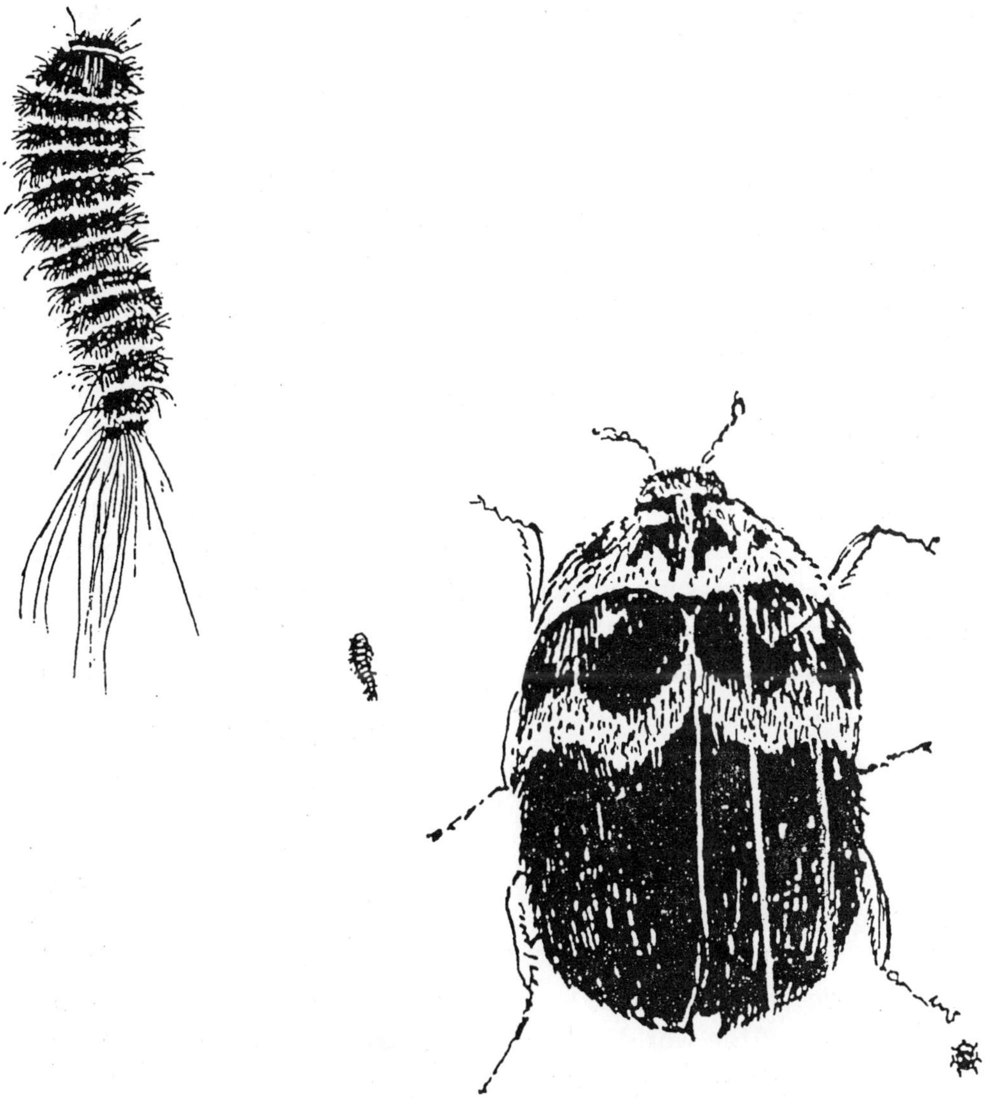

Larva and adult of the Carpet Beetle, *Attagenus gloriosae*.

days depending upon temperature and humidity. High humidity favours a longer adult life. The adult feeds on pollen and nectar of flowers (Walker, 1944).

The duration of the life cycle, from the time the egg is laid to the time the adult emerges from the pupa, is about 28 to 40 days at 28 to 30 degrees centigrade; 50 to 55 days at approximately 23 degrees centigrade.

The larvae of *Dermestes vulpinus* are used successfully by several natural history museums in the United States including the American Museum of Natural History in New York, the National Museum of Natural History at the Smithsonian Institution in Washington D.C., the Field Museum of Natural History in Chicago and the Peabody Museum of Natural History at Yale University in New Haven etc. for making osteological preparations. The Leather Beetle larvae do an excellent job of cleaning skeletons by their voracious feeding activity upon the dried and semi-dried fleshy matter, leaving bones and cartilages superbly cleaned and intact. They would eat up the flesh even of specimens that were previously preserved in alcohol. In these museums great care is taken in keeping these "Bug Houses" isolated, and often maintained far away from the museum, to prevent the possible spread of larvae into exhibition galleries and storage areas.

THE CARPET BEETLE

Several species of the genus *Attagenus* (Order: Coleoptera, Family: Dermestidae) have been described as Carpet Beetles. *Attagenus gloriosae* is one of the most common of the Carpet beetles found in India, harmful to museum collections. These are known to be confined mostly to the tropical humid regions of the world. *A. gloriosae* was first recorded in houses in Hawaii by Sharp (1855). According to Willcocks (1922, 1925) it is a common household pest in Egypt where the larvae feed on skins, furs, feathers, woolen goods etc. Kalshoven (1935) recorded it from Java in horse hair in store houses. Szent Ivany (1968) mentions that the larvae of *A. gloriosae* have been found damaging specimens of insects in New Guinea. The insect was introduced into England, according to Hinton (1945), during 1934 through cargoes coming from India.

The larvae of *A. gloriosae* were first collected by the author from inside old book-bindings in Hyderabad (Andhra Pradesh, India) and from woolen costumes in Baroda (Gujarat, India). The larvae thus collected were reared in the laboratory, their life history studied and feeding responses determined.

The female beetles oviposit on woolen fabrics. About fifty eggs are laid by the adult female. The incubation period varies from 8 to 12 days depending upon temperature. Between 30 to 32 degrees centigrade the eggs took and average of 8 days to hatch.

The Larva

The larvae are dark brown to black in colour and clothed with short scale-like appressed hairs and are provided with a tuft of long hairs at the end of the body. A full grown larva may reach nearly the size of 12 mm. in length and 2 to 3 mm. in breadth. The larvae moult a number of times, usually about seven. The duration of the larval period showed wide variations ranging from 120 to 160 days depending upon temperature and food. Reared on wool at about 32 degrees centigrade and 70% rH the larvae took an average of 126 days from the hatching of the egg to pupation. The larvae feed mostly on wool, but they also attack several other kinds of proteinaceous materials. The damage done by the larvae on woolen textiles is usually found in the form of scattered holes.

THE KHAPRA BEETLE

The Khapra Beetle, *Trogoderma granarlum* Everts is a serious pest of stored grains, mainly wheat. Believed to be indigenous to India, it has now

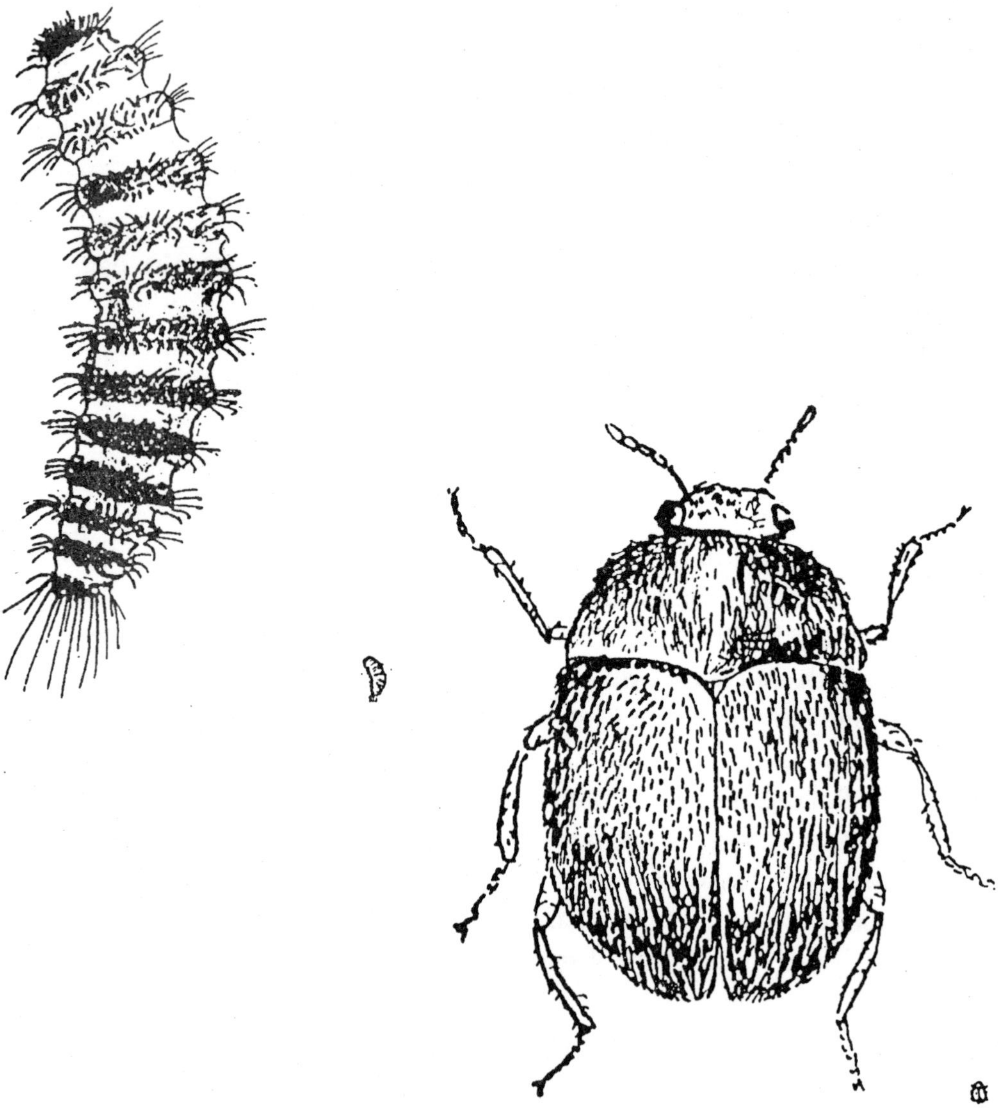

Larva and adult of the Khapra Beetle, *Trogoderma granarium*.

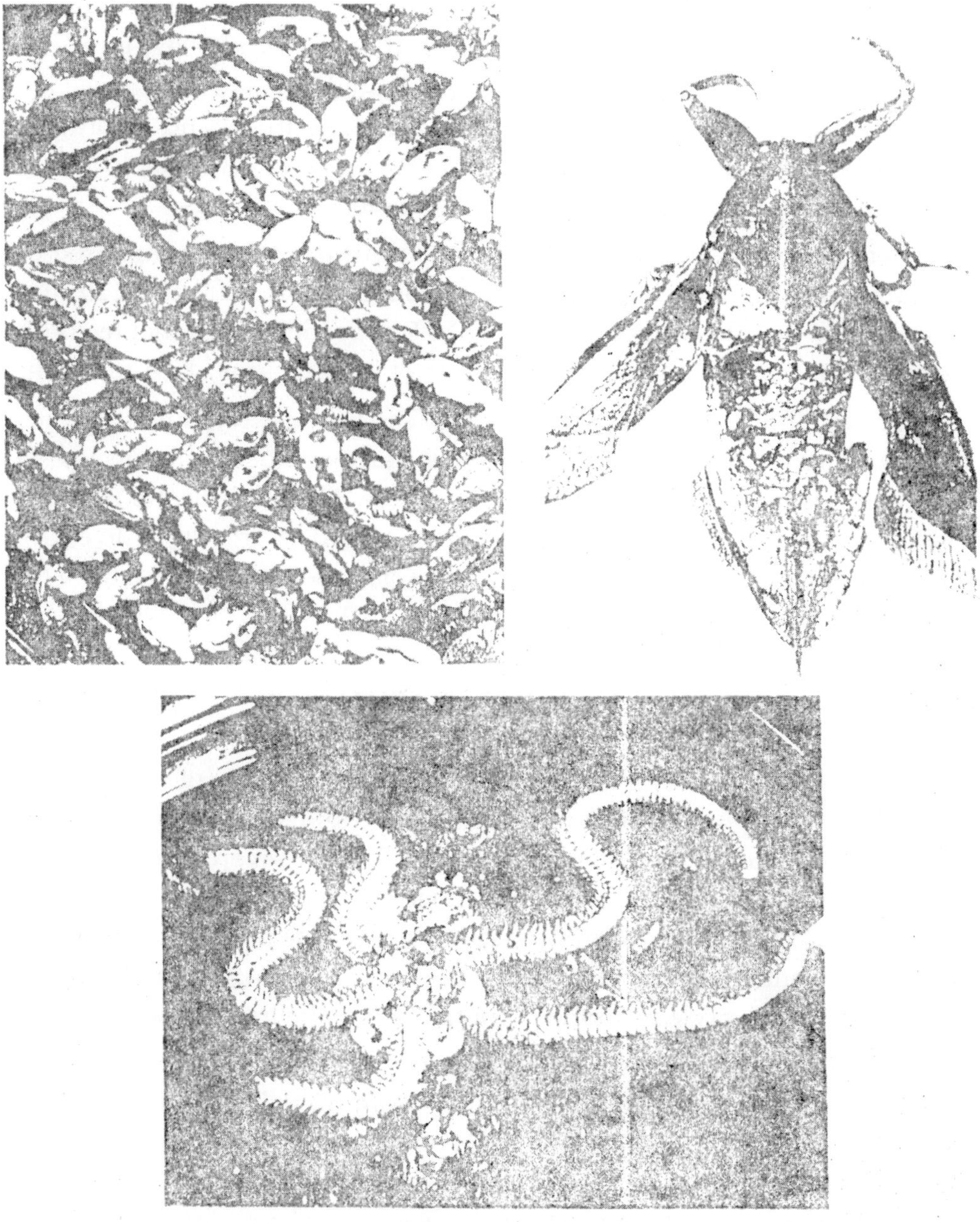

Khapra Beetle infestation on wheat, dried insect specimen and dried brittle star specimen.

acquired a world wide distribution. One of the earliest investigations on the biology of this dermestid beetle was that of Barnes and Grove (1916) in India. Since then several workers have contributed much to our knowledge of the biology and ecology of *Trogoderma* under natural and laboratory conditions. These studies have shown that it possesses remarkable ability to live under varied nutritional and environmental conditions.

Being a stored grain pest, *Trogoderma granarium* was supposed to be feared only in cereals and dried plant collections in museums. Hinton (1945) states that this is the only species of Dermestid beetles that feeds on vegetable products, being particularly fond of wheat, barley, rice and malt.

The adult female lays 45 to 100 eggs. The larvae are yellowish brown in colour and are clothed with hairs. The average size of a full grown larva is 2-3 mm. in length and 1-1.5 mm. in breadth. The adult beetle is small, averaging 1.8 to 3 mm. in length and 1 to 1.7 mm. in breadth. The entire duration of the life cycle from egg to adult was observed to range from 28 to 48 days.

CLOTHES MOTHS

There are several species of Clothes moths, the larvae of which cause extensive damage to woolen fabrics. Materials left undisturbed and neglected for a long time and stored in dark places are often severely damaged by them. These Lepidopterans are small, dusky brown or buff coloured and not over 10 to 12 mm. in length across the wings. The adult moth does not feed; their mouth parts are imperfectly developed. Damage is caused by the larvae and the life cycle is normally completed on the infested wool itself.

Clothes moths are distributed all over the world. The most common species are the Webbing Clothes Moth, *Tineola bisselliella*, and the Case-bearing Clothes Moth, *Tinea pellionella*. Other species include the Brown House Moth or False Clothes Moth, *Hofmannophila pseudospretella*, the White-shouldered House Moth, *Endrosis sarcitrella*, the Large Pale

Clothes Moth, *Tinea pallescentella*, the White Tipped Clothes Moth or Tapestry moth, *Trichophaga tapetzella* etc. Several of the above are reported to be found in Western Europe (Gradidge *et. al.*, 1976).The Webbing Clothes moth and the Case-baring Clothes moth are the most common wool destroying moths in the United States (Metcalf and Flint, 1939). The larvae of the Webbing clothes moths spin transparent fibres and while they feed produce a web like mass of silken threads upon the food material. On attaining maturity, the larvae spin silken cocoons in which are also incorporated bits of excrement and food and they pupate in them. The larvae of the Case-bearing Clothes moths spin portable cases in which they live.

Among the Clothes moths that damage fabrics in museums in India, it was observed that the most common pest is the Case-bearing Clothes moth, *Tinea pellionella* Linnaeus (Order: Lepidoptera; Family: Tineidae). It has been reported to be occurring in West and Central Asia, India, Ceylon, Japan, Australia, New Zealand, North America, North and South Africa and Europe (Hinton, 1945). The present survey of biodeterioration of Indian museums revealed that this species of clothes moth is a serious menace, particularly to woolen textiles and carpets as well as stuffed mammalian specimens. The author observed heavy damage to specimens of tigers, monkeys and cats in a museum in India, whose prolonged infestation has made the fur completely disappear, leaving the bare skins exposed. The feeding activity and subsequent loss of hair was found to be enormous in certain storage conditions where proper preventive care was not taken. Where left unnoticed, the textiles were raised to powder by larval activity and the quick succession of generations.

Apart from general descriptions of the insect by some authors and a paper by Cheema (1956), no detailed account of the life history and feeding habits of the insect in different temperature and humidity ranges was available. A detailed study of the biology and food preferences of the species was therefore undertaken. A description of the different stages of the insect along with the results of observations on the biology of the species is given below:

The female moth lays about 35 to 50 eggs. The egg when laid is pale white in colour, but soon becomes brownish white. It is oval in shape, slightly broader at one end and with longitudinal minute furrows on the surface observable only under the microscope. The average dimension of the egg is 0.5 mm. in length and 0.3 mm. in width.

Humidity did not seem to have any appreciable effect on the viability of the eggs. In contrast to the observations in Dermestid beetles, temperature ranges between 25 and 28 degrees centigrade were found to be more suitable for the development of the eggs of *tinea pellionella.*

The Larva

The freshly hatched larva is pale white in colour and measures a maximum of about 1mm. in length and 0.2mm. in width. It is interesting to watch the activities of the larva under a binocular microscope. For about a day after emergence the larva simply wanders around on the fabric. After this it settles down and starts constructing a case around its body. The larva starts spinning silk threads by a secretion from its mouth which dries in air and a case of silk is made initially. Now it cuts small bits of the wool fibre and pastes it on the case. This activity goes on for about 24 hours until the case is complete. After the case is built the larva moves around with it (hence the name 'Case-bearing Clothes Moth') and starts feeding on the wool. As the larva grows the case enlarges. The larva is capable of making a complete turn within the case which enables it to feed on the material at either end without having to alter the position of the case. While crawling the larva protrudes outside the case to about half its length and holds on to the surface of the fabric by means of hooks present at the tip of the thoracic legs. When inactive, the larva remains inside the case. The fully grown larva

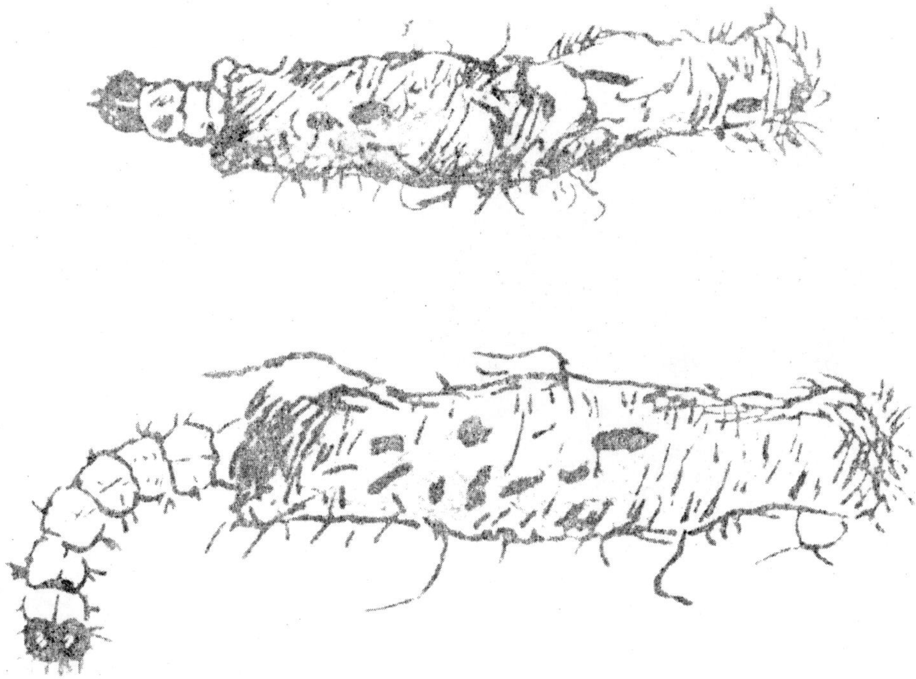

Larvae of Case-bearning Clothes Moth, *Tinea pellionella*.

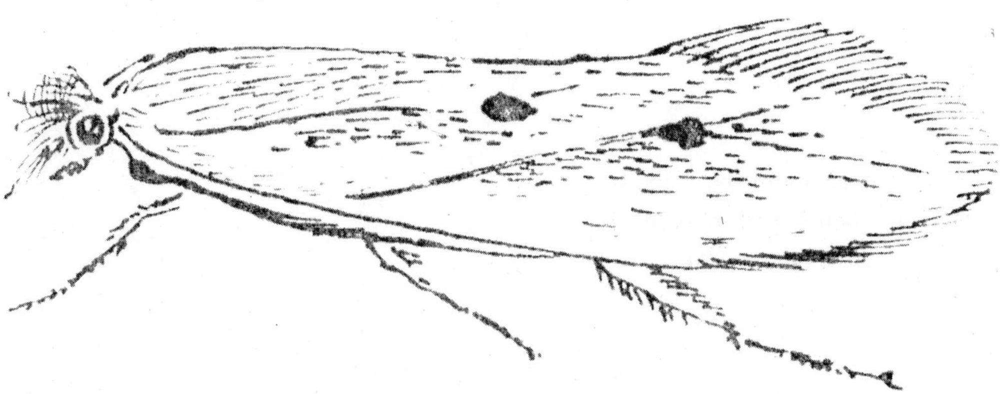

Case-bearing Clothes Moth, *Tinea pellionella* (Adult).

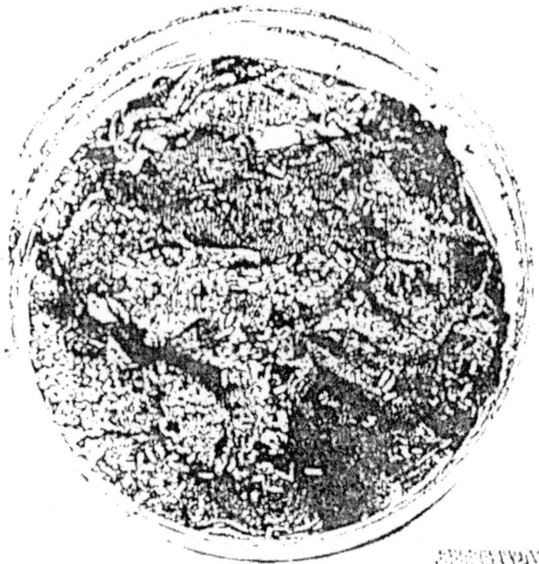

Culture of the case-bearing clothes Moth, *Tinea pellionella*.

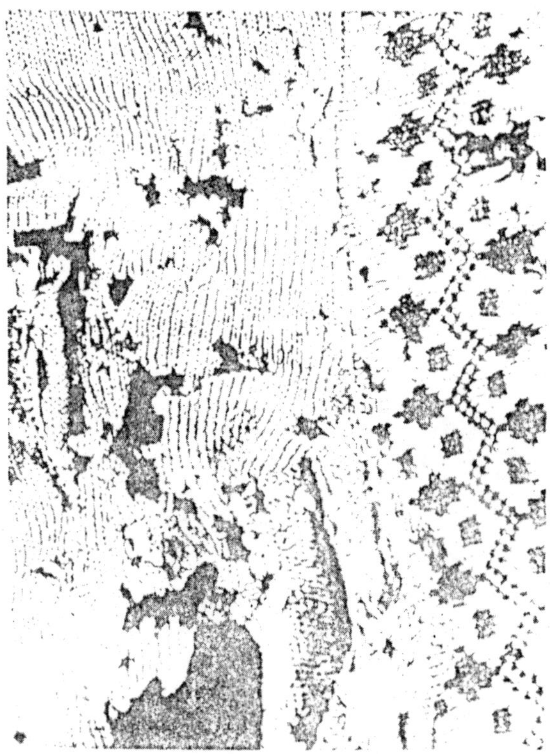

A woolen garment damaged by the Case-bearing Clothes Moth, *Tinea pellionella*.

measures from 4 mm. to 7.5 mm. in length and 1.1 to 1.35mm in width (without the case).

The shortest larval periods were observed within a temperature range of 25 to 28 degrees centigrade and relative humidity of about 70%. During the course of the study it was also observed that larvae are usually capable of building another case if the original one is stripped off.

The Pupa

It was observed that fully grown larvae leave the food material and crawl along the walls of the container and if possible leave the culture medium in search of quiet places to pupate. They get into any material nearby for the purpose but do not cause any damage to the substances at this stage. There is a pre-pupal period when they fix their cases, close one end with fine silken thread and remain inactive within. The pre-pupal period is of 4 to 5 days duration. At the end of the pre-pupal period, the larva casts off its last larval skin within the case and pupates. Outwardly there are no indications to show that it has pupated. The pupal period is about 8 to 10 days.

The Adult

After metamorphosis, the newly formed adult emerges out of its pupal cover. The anterior half of the pupa protrudes from the case at the time of emergence and the pupal shell remains half way out from the case after emergence of the adult.

The adult is light brown in colour with three dark spots forming the apices of a triangle on each fore-wing. The hind wings are yellowish brown in colour, shiny, and fringed with long slender scales at the posterior margin. The average size in sitting position of the adult is about 6to 10 mm. in length and about 12 mm. wingspread from one end to the other. The males are slightly smaller than the females and more active fliers; females are sluggish and fly only for short distances. Mating takes place within 12 hours after emergence.

The total period required for completion of the life cycle of the larvae with wool as larval nutrition was found to be about 40 to 50 days within temperature ranges of about 25 to 28 degrees centigrade and relative humidity ranging between 70 and 90%. The adults do not feed. Cheema (1956) reports that the damage to fabrics maintained in darkness was significantly greater than damage to those maintained alternatively in light and darkness.

Because of the short duration of the life cycle of this species of Clothes Moth, the number of generations in a year is far more than that of Dermestid beetle: There are 3 to 4 generations in a year. The damage done to woolen fabrics is enormous due to this quick succession of generations and the voracious feeding activity of the larvae.

Other Minor Pests

There are many more insect pests that attack organic materials in museum collections. Only the most important among them have been discussed above. A few more species of museum pests, perhaps of lesser importance remain to be mentioned. They are considered minor pests because they were not found as frequently as the others.

The Drug-store Beetle

The Drug-store beetle, *Stegobium paniceum* (Linnaeus) belonging to the Coleopteran family *Anobiidae* is a stored products pest of the world wide distributions. The adult beetle, 2.2 to 3.7mm. in length is reddish brown in colour. The larva, cylindrical and 'C' shaped, 3 to 4mm. long is whitish brown in colour. It is reported to feed on materials such as bread, dried

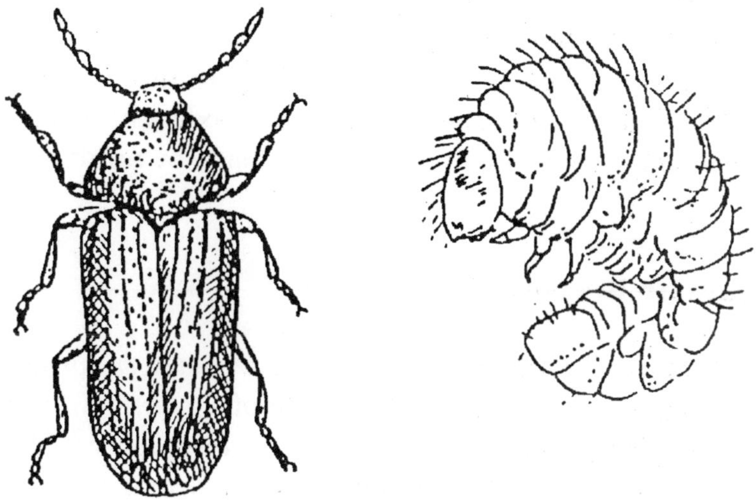

Drug-store Beetle, *Stegobium paniceum*.

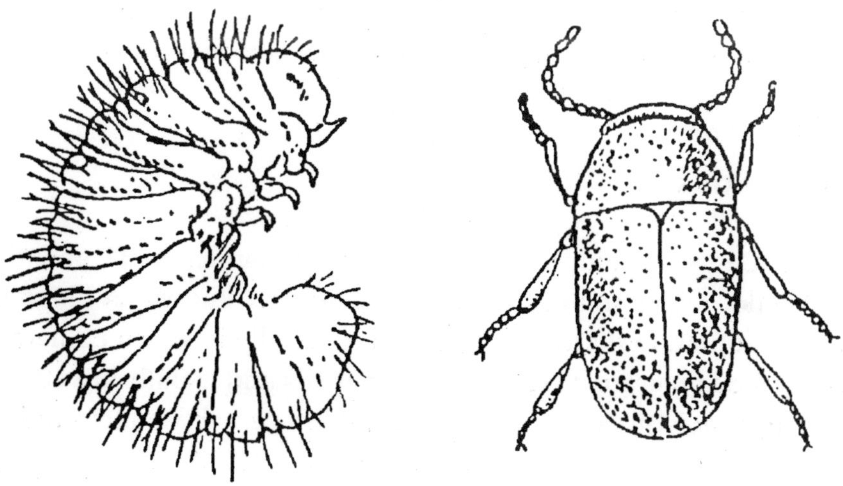

Cigarette Beetle, *Lasioderma Serricorne*.

cereals, spices, stored food, books, leather and cork as well as botanical and insect specimens (Kingsolver, 1981).

The drug-store beetle, a member of the furniture beetle family has become adapted to a diet of starch containing foods. The round exit holes made by the larvae look similar to the holes made by furniture beetles on timber.

The Cigarette Beetle

The Cigarette or Tobacco beetle, *Lasioderma serricorne* Fabricius (Family: Anobiidae) believed to be a native of Egypt, now cosmopolitan in distribution, is a most destructive pest of stored tobacco. It is a small squat beetle, light brown in colour and two to three mm. in length. It is also said to be a serious pest of books causing damage to bindings and paper. Furniture upholstered with flax or straw is also attacked severely. One of the remarkable feeding habits of this insect reported by Mallis (1964) is that it can feed on pyrethrum powder strong enough to kill cockroaches. Merril (1948) states that it feeds on dried flowers making it known as 'herbarium beetle'. Flint and Mc. Cauley (1937) note that this insect also can damage silk.

Flour Beetles

The 'Confused Flour Beetle', *Tribolium confusum* H and the Red Flour Beetle, *Tribolium castaneum* H, generally known as Flour Beetles are cosmopolitan in distribution, found especially in warm climates. They generally feed on grain dust and milled cereals and usually are attracted to flour of high moisture content. They also infest cereal products and grocery

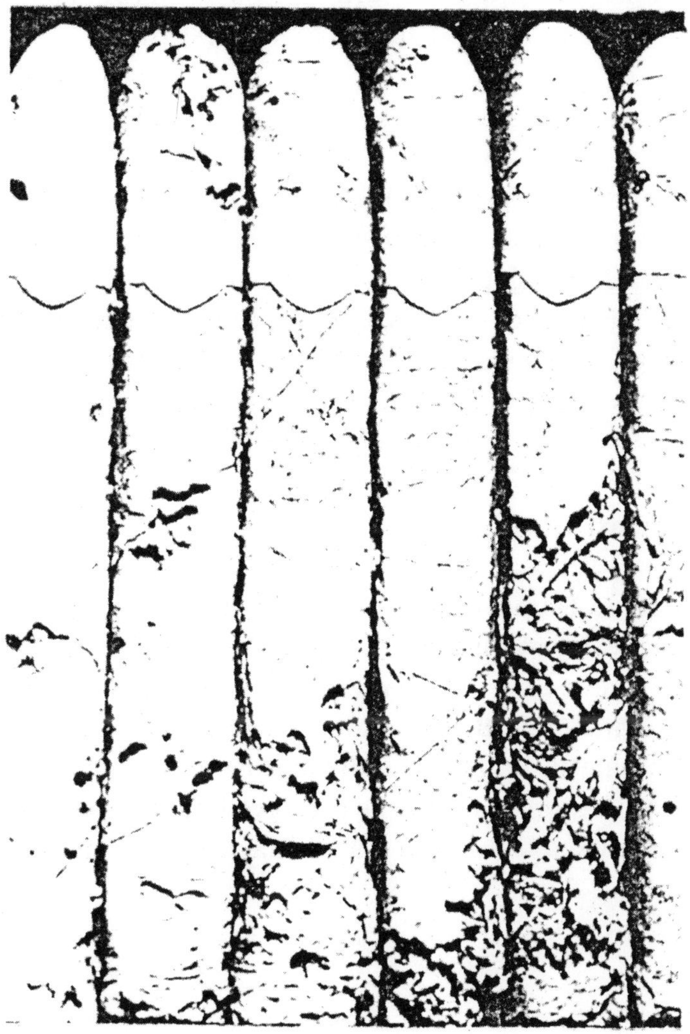

Cigars damaged by Tabocco Beetle, *Lasioderma serricorne* (Courtesy, Collins Guide to Wild Life in House and Home).

stores. In India these insects have been noticed as museum pests infesting herbarium collections and dried entomological specimens.

Spider Beetles

Spider Beetles belonging to the family *Ptinidae* are minor museum pests feeding on animal skins, stuffed birds, herbarium specimens, stored cereals and dried entomological collections. One of the species observed in museum collection in India is *Gibbium psylloides* (Czemp). It is because of their long legs, antennae and short body with hairs resembling small spiders that they are called 'spider beetles'. It is not of much significance in Indian museums compared to dermestid beetles.

Redlegged Ham Beetle

The Redlegged Ham Beetle, *Nercobia rufipes* De Geer is reported as pest in Freze-Dry Laboratories in U.S.A. (Edwards and Bell, 1981). The adult beetle is dark metallic blue in colour with red legs. The larva is cylindrical, white, with dark brown head. The adult measures 3.5 to 7mm and the larva 9 to 10 mm. in length. Both the adults and larvae are known to damage dead animal flesh. Animal specimens preserved by the technique of freeze drying contains dried animal flesh that is attacked by the insect.

Ants, Bees and Wasps

Ants, bees and wasps also deserve mention in connection with the biodeterioration of museum materials, even though they are not as injurious as other pests. In India there are several kinds of ants that infest food products, attack fabrics and other organic materials. Some species of ants, a few wasps and the Carpenter bees are reported to have caused damage to cultural property in the tropics. Dried entomological collectons are often eaten by ants if they are not properly preserved and protected.

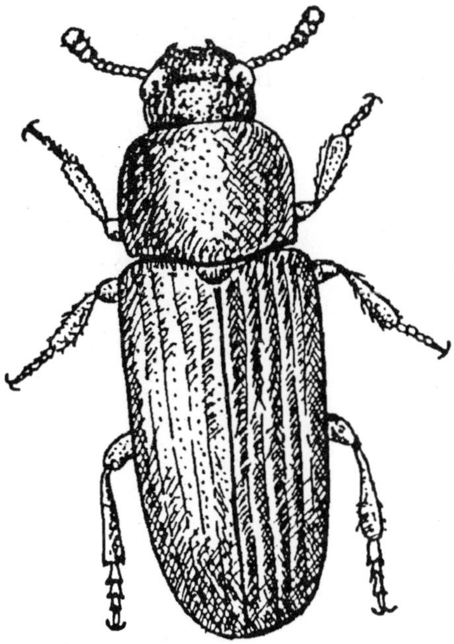

Red Flour Beetle, *Tribolium castaneum*.

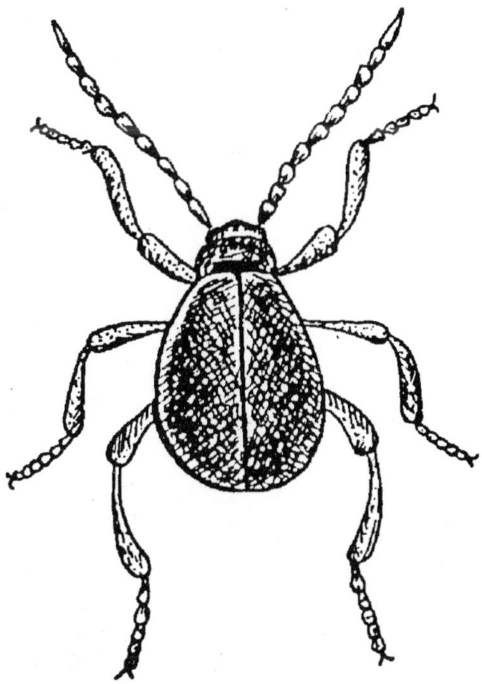

Spider Beetle, *Gibbium psylloides*.

Wasps cannot attack museum materials, but do cause a nuisance by constructing their earthen nests on wooden sculptures, display furniture etc. The Carpenter bees bore into structural timber.

For further information on insect pests attention of the reader is invited to an excellent reference listing of museum pests compiled by Richard Beauchamp, John Kingsolver and Thomas Parker (1981).

Apart from insects thee are other animals that cause biodeterioration of museum materials where conditions are favourable. These include rodents (rats and mice) birds and bats.

Chapter III

STUDIES ON THE FEEDING RESPONSES OF CERTAIN INSECT PESTS

The success of an organism largely depends upon its capacity to compromise with the availability of food and the environment. Several of the pests described in Chapter II possess characteristics that demonstrate their capacity for such adaptations. They have a remarkable ability to thrive on a wide variety of food materials. Varied food habits are considered highly beneficial for the species in maintaining itself in a wide spectre of environmental circumstances.

As far as pest control in museums is concerned, an understanding of the above characteristics of the insects is vital. It may often by necessary to protect a wide variety of materials the pest is likely to attack, even if the infestation is noticed only on one type of material. For example, if attack by *Anthrenus flavipes* is detected, say, on woolen carpets, it immediately calls for preventive measures to be taken also with respect to collections of hair, fur, feather, taxidermy specimens, entomological specimens and similar other proteinaceous materials. Such precautionary measures can be taken only if information is available about the type of materials that *Anthrenus flavipes* is likely to attack. Unfortunately, information of this kind is not easily available in the case of several museum pests.

Experiments on the feeding responses of some of the insects were conduced using various kinds of food materials. The feeding preferences of *Anthrenus flavipes, Attagenus gloriosae* and *Tinea pellionella* were assessed in this study. The results of the study indicated the types of materials these insects are most likely to attack.

Feeding Responses of the Furniture Carpet Beetle *(Anthrenus flavipes)*

Several experiments were conducted to assess the nutritional requirements and the range of feeding activity of *Anthrenus flavipes,* the Furniture Carpet Beetle. Samples of different organic materials represented in usual museum collections were taken in the same quantities by weight and kept in Petri-dishes. Twenty larvae each were introduced in them, and maintained at a temperature of 32±1 degrees centigrade in an incubator. The larvae released were 10 days old, fed on wool since emergence. These young larvae were selected for the experiment because grown up ones have the capacity to undergo prolonged starvation if food is not agreeable, thereby making it difficult to obtain reliable results on feeding responses, rate of mortality etc.

Table I: Feeding Responses of the larvae of Purniture carpet Beetle (Anthremnus flavipes)

Diet	Ist week	2nd week	3rd week	4th week	6th week	8th week	12th week
Mammalian hair	actively feeding	actively feeding	actively feeding	actively feeding	2 adults emerged	all emergd into adults; eggs laid.	New generation of larvae active
Woolen textile	actively feeding	actively feeding	actively feeding	actively feeding	3 adults emerged	all emergd into adults; eggs laid.	New generation of larvae active
Feather	actively feeding	actively feeding	actively feeding	actively feeding	2 adults emerged	all emergd into adults; eggs laid.	New generation of larvae active
Buffalo horn	actively feeding	actively feeding	actively feeding	actively feeding	5 adults emerged	all emergd into adults; eggs laid.	New generation of larvae active
Dried insects	actively feeding	actively feeding	actively feeding	actively feeding	4 adults emerged	all emergd into adults; eggs laid.	New generation of larvae active
Incompletely cleaned skeleton	actively feeding on dried meat	actively feeding on dried meat	actively feeding on dried meat	actively feeding on dried meat	3 adults emerged	all emergd into adults; eggs laid.	New generation of larvae active
Leather (chrome tanned)	No feeding	No feeding	5 dead	12 dead	all dead	-	-
Silk fabric	No feeding	No feeding	6 dead	10 dead	all dead	-	-
Fish skin (dried)	trying to feed	no feeding	3 dead	6 dead	all dead	-	-
Herbarium	no feeding	no feeding	4 dead	12 dead	all dead	-	-
Cereal (Wheat)	no feeding	no feeding	2 dead	6 dead	all dead	-	-
Palm leaf	no feeding	no feeding	3 dead	15 dead	all dead	-	-

Feeding activity of the larvae were recorded every week and the emergence of adults and mortality in each case were noted. The results are shown in Table 1.

The results show that hair, wool, fur, feather and horn (primarily kerationous in nature) are the favourite food materials among museum collections. They do not feed on dried echinoderms or sponges. Chrome tanned leather is not attacked, possibly because of the presence of Chromic oxide. Silk was also found to be unaffected. Dried insects are voraciously devoured and even the hard chitinous parts are consumed by the insect larvae. Plant products are not attacked by the larvae.

Feeding Responses of the Carpet Beetle *(Attagenus gloriosae)*

Wool was found to be the most preferred food of this insect. It was an observation of the presence of the larvae of this insect inside book-bindings that induced the present study. When larvae were found within book-bindings, freely moving around in the larval galleries of *Gastrallus indicus,* it was though that Attagenus was present there as a scavenger feeding on larval and pupal exuviae as well as the dead adults of the Book-Worm beetle. But, the present study in which the larvae were found to feed and grown quite normally on book-bindgings composed of vegetable tanned leather shows that they are independently capable of causing damage to such materials.

The feeding responses of the larvae on various materials were determined. The method followed was the same as in the case of the previous experiment.

The results of the study (Table II) show that several kinds of mammalian hair and feathers of birds also favour their growth as much as woolen fabrics, demonstrating the potential threat of this insect to taxidermy collections in natural history museums. Chrome tanned leather was found unaffected in this case. But, vegetable tanned leather is easily attacked. Silk fabrics and

Table II: Feeding Responses of the larvae of Carpet Beetle (Attagenus gloriosae)

Diet	Ist week	2nd week	3rd week	4th week	5th week	6th week	7th week	8th week
Mammalian hair	actively feeding	actively feeding	actively feeding	actively feeding	actively feeding	actively feeding	actively feeding	actively feeding grown in size
Woolen Fabric	actively feeding	actively feeding	actively feeding	actively feeding	actively feeding	actively feeding	actively feeding	actively feeding grown in size
Feather	actively feeding	actively feeding	actively feeding	actively feeding	actively feeding	actively feeding	actively feeding	actively feeding grown in size
Book-binding (vegetable tanned leather)	actively feeding	actively feeding	actively feeding	actively feeding	actively feeding	actively feeding	actively feeding	actively feeding grown in size
Leather (Chrome tanned)	trying to feed	trying to feed	No feeding	No feedind	2 dead	4dead	all dead	-
Silk Fabric	trying to feed	some initial feeding	No feeding	No feedind	3 dead	all dead	-	
Cotton Fabric	no feeding	inactive	3 dead	all dead	-	-	-	-
Herbarium	trying to feed	slight feeding	no feeding	1 dead	2 dead	4 dead	5 dead	-
Palm leaf	no feeding	no feeding	2 dead	4 dead	5 dead	-	-	-

herbarium specimens of plants showed initial damage due to the larvae, but the larvae could not sustain themselves on these materials.

Feeding Responses of the Case-bearing Clothes Moth *(Tinea pellionella)*

Several sets of experiments were conducted in the case of the larvae of the Case-bearing Clothes moth, *Tinea pellionella.* In the first case, freshly hatched larvae, after they had completed case building (i.e., 2 days old), were released on the materials selected for the study. Until the 5th day observations were made daily and from then on at intervals of five days.

No feeding was noticed in silk, cotton, fur and dried star fishes and most of the larvae died by the 10th day. Some survived a few more days, but ultimately died before the 15th day on account of starvation. Those released on feather, leather and dried insects as well as dried fish showed some initial feeding activity but the mortality rate increased progressively and most of them died by the 15th day. Those released on woolen fabric and fur were the only ones that survived and were observed to feed actively and grow in size

This experiment categorically shows that wool (General hair) is the best medium for the growth of *Tinea pellionella.* But it was thought desirable to find out the feeding responses of mature larvae as well on different materials, to discover whether they are capable of feeding on any other material. It was thought that it is likely that freshly hatched larvae are unable to adjust immediately to a new diet while mature ones may be able to. With this objective in mind the second experiment was designed and carried out.

In this experiment 30 days old mature larvae were taken and released on various materials. It was almost a repetition of the previous experiment but with mature larvae, instead of freshly hatched larvae. The feeding materials used were the same.

Table III: Feeding Responses of the larvae of Case-bearing Clothes Moth (Tinea pellionella)

Feeding Material	Ist day	2nd day	3rd day	4th day	5th day	10th day	15th day
Wool	actively feeding	actively feeding	feeding growing	feeding growing	feeding growing	feeding growing	feeding growing
Silk	No feeding	larvae inactive	2 dead	3 dead	3 dead	6 dead	all dead
Cotton	no feeding	inactive	4 dead	all dead	-	-	-
Feather	trying to feed	slight feeding	slight feeding	no feeding 3 dead	6 dead	all dead	-
Leather	trying to feed	feeding	feeding	no feeding	4 dead	6 dead	all dead
Fur	Poor feeding	feeding	feeding growing	feeding growing	feeding growing	feeding growing	feeding growing
Dried insects	trying to feed	slight feeding	no feeding	3 dead	5 dead	7 dead	all dead
Dried Star fish	no feeding	4 dead	6 dead	7 dead	9 dead	all dead	-
Dried fish	tries to feed	slight feeding	no feeding	3 dead	6 dead	7 dead	all dead

The results (Table V) show that a complete development with normal growth and egg laying as well as repetition of subsequent generations of *Tinea pellionella* is possible only on wool and fur. Nevertheless, mature larvae are also capable of feeding upon other materials life leather, feather, dried fish, dried insects etc., and some could even complete their life cycle on these materials although the rate of egg laying and progression of subsequent generations were severely hampered.

A third set of experiments with *Tinea pellionella* was conducted wherein the larvae were ripped out of their cases, made naked and released on a few different types of materials. This experiment was done to find out their reactions on wool, silk and cotton and to see whether they are capable of re-building their cases. Those released on wool readily built new cases within 24 hours and started regular feeding activity. Those on cotton wandered around and some of them ultimately built cases with the help of silken threads secreted by the larvae themselves; but, they did not show any feeding activity and ultimately died. Larvae that were released on silk made use of the fibrous ends of the silk fabric and built up cases around them. They too did not feed and finally died within about 14 days. During this experiment it was also noticed that some of the larvae tried to feed on the woolen fibres present on the case of other larvae in the goup.

In the fourth set of experiments with *Tina pellionella* some mature pupae were introduced on silk in order to find out whether the adults that emerge would show normal fecundity and whether the larvae that hatch out of the eggs laid would feed and develop on silken fabrics. Several adults emerged in due course of time, mated and the females laid eggs. The number of eggs was comparatively less than the usual number laid on wool (only 10 to 12 eggs per adult female were laid). The incubation period was normal and the larvae emerged as usual. The newly emerged larvae moved around for a day and did not utilize silk for case building. The case building activity was delayed for two more days after which it was found that the larvae had concentrated on the pupal cases of the adults and started utilising the woolen fibres present on them for building their cases. Though several

Table IV: Feeding Responses of the mature larvae of the Case bearing Clothes Moth (Tinea pellionella)

Feeding Material	Ist week	2nd week	3rd week	4th week	5th week	6th week
Wool	actively feeding	feeding growing	feeding growing	4 pupae	4 adults 6 pupae	all adults; eggs laid; some hatched into larvae
Silk	tries to feed feeding	no feeding inactive	3 dead	8 dead	all dead	-
Cotton	no feeding	2 dead	5 dead	all dead	-	- -
Feather	tries to feed	some feeding	2 dead	5 dead	all dead	-
Leather	tries to feed	some feeding	2 dead others feeding	4 dead others feeding	6 dead others feeding	2 adults emerged others dead
Fur	actuely feeding	feeding growing	feeding growing	feeding growing	5 pupae	5 pupae 5 adults
Dried insects	tries to feed	some feeding	some feeding 2 dead	5 dead	7 dead	3 adults emerged
Dried Star fish	no feeding	3 dead	5 dead	all dead	-	-
Dried fish	tries to feed	feeding	feeding	3 dead, some feeding	5 dead 2 adults emerged	6 larvae dead; 2 more adults emerged (total 4 adults)

larvae succeeded in building their cases, if not completely, with the fibres present on the pupal cases, within another 10 days all the larvae died on account of not having enough wool for either case making or feeding.

This experiment and the observations made convincingly show that *Tinea pellionella* will not attack silk as it cannot survive on a diet of silk. They could thrive on wool which is the favourite diet. They may not be able to feed and continue their generations on any other material than wool as seen from the present studies, but they could feed on other keratinous substances like feather, dried fish etc. and occasionally on leather.

The present feeding response studies were limited to only three pest species. Similar studies on other pests is bound to provide us with valuable information on the food preferences of other insects responsible for causing biodeterioration of objects in museums.

Chapter IV

BIODETERIORATION OF CULTURAL PROPERTY

Having dealt with organisms responsible for biodeterioration and their characteristics in the previous two chapters, this one examines specific problems with regard to various kinds of cultural property consisting of paper, books and manuscripts, wood and wood products, leather objects, textiles, stone, wall paintings etc. Effective control of biodeterioration depends upon an understanding of the properties of the affected material, characteristics of the organism that has infested it, and the right kind of treatment (chemical or otherwise) to combat the problem without endangering the material itself. It is therefore necessary to consider individually the question of biodeterioration of each type of material.

PAPER, BOOKS AND MANUSCRIPTS

The chief constituent of paper is cellulose. Some papers are made from wood pulp while others are made from cotton and linen rags, straw, waste paper etc. all of which contain cellulose. Many non-fibrous materials are also used in manufacturing paper. These include lime, sodium silicate, sulphur, chlorine, calcium carbonate, talc, clay,alum, rosin, pigments and dye stuffs, ssoda ash, caustic soda, starch, gelatine,casein or other sizing materials. Essentially the manufacture of paper involves separation and purification of the cellulose fibres and production of thin sheets from it. Several chemicals are added for bleaching purposes and other non-fibrous materials used depending upon the type of paper to be made. The raw materials and chemicals that go into the composition of paper play a predominant role in its permanence or deterioration. Biological deterioration of paper, books and other archival materials is a problem of great seriousness for museums, libraries and archives all over the world. This is brought about by bacteria, fungi, insects, rodents etc.

Bacteria

A large variety of bacteria associated with paper have been studied by many investigators. Although aerobic bacteria may be involved in deterioration of paper, they do not play as predominent a role as do the fungi. Bacteria require extremely humid or moist surrounding to grow. They cause serious deterioration to cellulose in growing plants, cellulose present in sewage and garbage disposal, timber, pulp and paper industry etc. Under normal conditions bacterial decomposition of paper is very unlikely. Since bacteria play an important role in the degradation of cellulose in general, the micro-biology of cellulose decomposition has been studied by many. These studies, however, are not directly relevant to the deterioration of paper in museums, libraries and archives.

Fausta Gallo (1963) refers to damage caused by schizomycetes such as *Cellvibrio, Cellfalcicula* and *Cytophaga* which have a cellulose dissolving capacity The degradation brought about to books in humid conditions is mainly due to the binding glue used. Similarly the presence of grease and saliva on paper (through the bad habit of turning paper by a finger moistened with saliva) may induce bacterial growth on paper. Studies by Walksman (1954) also refer to the above mentioned bacterial species as destructive to paper.

Since bacterial decomposition of paper, books and manuscripts is not a matter of serious concern for museums, libraries and archives, and as most of the fungicides when used act also as effective bactericides, no further discussion on bacterial attack on paper is considered necessary here.

Fungus Growth on Paper

More than a hundred varieties of fungi are known to attack paper and paper materials. These fungi have a remarkable cellulose dissolving capacity. It is well known that cellulose provides a satisfactory medium for fungus growth. Staining and weakening of paper are the obvious results of fungal activity. The growth of fungi on paper also adds to the acidic content of paper which in due course of time accelerates chemical decomposition of paper. The fungi growing on paper usually produce black, brown or yellow spots and some may even be colourless.

Chromatic alterations on paper on account of fungus growth may depend upon several factors. Fausta Gallo (1963) summarises these factors as follows:

1. Type of paper and the chemical processes it has undergone during manufacture.
2. The conditions under which the infection occurred. (atmospheric humidity, moisture in the paper, temperature etc.)
3. The length of action of the fungal species (Long or short period of latent infection).
4. The co-existence of several fungal species.

5. The possible presence of traces of iron, copper or other metals in the paper.
6. The acidity of the paper.

As one or several of these factors may be responsible for discolouration, it is impossible to establish the identity of the fungus based only on that. It often is necessary to identify the species by making pure cultures with the help of the spores available. Beckwith and co-workers (1940) have isolated nearly 55 species of fungi from old books and manuscripts belonging to the genera, *Alternaria, monillia, Aspergillus, Penicillium, Mucor, Stemphylium, Hormodendrum, Fusarium, Chaetomium* and *Byssochlamys*. It is likely that the spores of some of the common fungi are present on almost all kinds of materials or may be accidentally present on paper.

Studies by Waksman (1940) show the presence on paper of fungi belonging to the genera *Chaetomium, Myxotrichium, Eidemella, Aspergillus, Acrostalagmus, Stemphylium, Alternaria, Stysanus* and *Fusarium*. These are all cellulose decomposing organisms and some are also pigment forming bringing about staining of paper.

Foxing, a characteristic rusty-brown spotted discolouration is said to be associated with fungus growth. Beckwith *et. al.* (1940) observes that foxing or brown-spotting of paper is associated at least partly with fungus growth, but points out that it may also be due to the presence of iron. According to him the organic acids secreted by fungi in the course of their metabolic processes react with the traces of iron present in paper forming salts that decompose into oxides and hydroxides of iron. These are responsible for the rusty-brown discolouration. Ambler and Finney (1957) have shown that micro-organisms are directly responsible for foxing. They develop because of the presence of glue and starch forming hygroscopic areas on paper in which the water soluble products of the decomposition of cellulose accumulate. These assume a brown-red colour in damp surroundings.

Opinions are varied on the causes, nature and mechanism of foxing and the available information is inadequate for making any definite statement in this respect.

Niuksha (1960), after studying the percentage of cellulose degraded in laboratory cultures, observes that the most important paper mycelia that show a marked cellulose dissolving activity are: *Penicillium, Paecilomyces Varioti, Chaetomium, Aspergillus Versicolour, Aspergillus Flarus, Trichoderma lignorum, T. koningi, Sporotrichium bombycimum, S. polysporum. Haolographium fuligineum etc.*

Flieder (1969), based on her work at the Laboratoire de Cryptogamie of the French National Museum of Natural History in Paris, reports the presecnce of several species of *Alternaria, Aspergillus, Botrytrichium, Chaetomium, Cladosporium, Curvularia, Epicoccus, Fusarium, Memnoniella, Myrotheceum, Penicillium, Neurospora and Pullularia* causing microbial deterioration of paper.

Extensive studies carried out on fungi associated with book collections in the Lenin Library, Moscow by Rybakova (1953) refer to the presence of *Aspergillus* (11 SPECIES) *Acrostalagmus Cephalosporium, Fusarium, Papulospora, Sporotrichium, Torula* and *Trichothecium* (one species each), *Penicillium* (23 species), *Stachysotrys* and *Stemphylium* (7 species each) and *Trichoderma* (14 species).

Further work in the Lenin Library on mould species and their injurious effects on book materials by Belyakova (1958) provides valuable information on the relative contribution to damage by various species of fungi. These studies led to the identification of 59 species of fungi deleterious to books. An interesting outcome of this study is the observation that damage caused to paper and books by fungi varies according to the composition of paper. Out of 349 mould infected books examined, it was found that 48.7% were printed on rag paper, 23.5% on rag paper mixed with ground wood or cellulose pulp, 16.2% on paper made of cellulose pulp mixed with ground wood, 7.5% on paper made of cellulose pulp and 5.1% on ground wood paper.

The fungi responsible for greatest cellulose destroying activity are identified as those belonging to the genera *Chetomium, Stachybotrys, Sporotrichium, Stemphylium, Penicillium, Aspergillus, Trichoderma, Botryotrichium, Haptographium, Rhonotrichum* and *Stephanoma.*

Belyakova's studies also confirm the general observation that the book cover is more frequently attacked by moulds. This is because of the higher content of glue in the cover than in other parts of the book, and because the cover materials are more hygroscopic. More moisture from the atmosphere is readily absorbed by this external part of the book. The leaves of the book nearest to the cover and edges of pages are also more exposed to the environment. Thus, there is more fungal damage in those areas than on the centre pages. The starch and gelatin used as sizing material for rag paper also attract fungus growth, whereas rosin is not a nutrient medium. Studies in the Lenin Library also show that *Aspergillus* and *Pencillium* are the predominant paper attacking species of fungi. This corresponds to the situation obtained in India also.

Studies conducted by the author on the isolation, culture and identification of fungi from old paper manuscripts in India showed the presence of the following fungi:

Aspergillus niger	*Curvularia tetramera*
Aspergillus glaucus	*Curvularia maculans*
Aspergillus flavus	*Trichoderma album*
Alternaria humicola	*Trichoderma lignorum*
Alternaria malvae	*Trichoderma glaucum*
Pencillium rubrum	*Fusarium clamydosporum*
Pencillium funicolosum	*Fusarium moniliformae*
Pencillium Chrysogenum	*Cladosporium herbarum*

Prevention and Control of Fungus Growth

One of the first considerations for prevention and control of fungus growth on paper should be the maintenance of a proper environment, one that will not allow fungus spores to germinate and grow. Spores are present everywhere, but they can grow on materials only when a certain amount of humidity is available and at a suitable temperature. The control of temperature and humidity at a level that does not allow spore germination and growth of fungi, therefore, is of paramount importance. Temperatures above 85°F and relative humidity above 70% are ideal for fungi to thrive. Maintenance of a temperature range of 70 to 75°F and relative humidity of 45-55% is, therefore, recommended for the storage and display of books, paper and manuscripts. Temperature is not so crucial as is humidity. Some fungi like *Aspergillus niger* grow under low temperatures found in refrigerators. In tropical humid conditions where air conditioning of libraries and manuscripts storage areas is not feasible for financial or other reasons, efforts should be made to bring down humidity by using moisture abosorbing materials like silica gel, calcium chloride etc.

Use of Fungicides

No single fungicide is likely to possess all the properties required to destroy or inhibit the growth of all the different species of fungi that may grow on paper. Considerable work has been done by many investigators on the use of fungicides on paper. though most of it is confined to the commercial uses of paper. Many of the commercial fungicides are highly chlorinated chemicals which may not be suitable for use on paper, because they may eventually break down and produce small traces of hydrochloric acid, detrimental to paper. Some chlorinated organic chemicals can however, be used in very small concentrations with great care often along with a neutralizing agent to negate possible damage due to acidity.

Prevention and control of fungus growth on paper involve several lines of action. These include use of fungus repellent chemicals in storage areas to prevent mould spores and use of fungicides either as sprays, applications of fumigants. More than anything else, the control of temperature and humidity is important to ensure environmental conditions not condusive to mould growth.

Langwel (1957) recommends the following methods for prevention of fungus growth on paper under appropriate conditions:

(1) Application of Salicylanilide (available in U.K. under the trade name "Shirlan") either in a weak alkaline, aqueous solution or in a a non-aqueous medium. He suggests a concentration of about 0.1% by weight of the fabric of paper. It is colourless and odourless and not likely to alter the appearance of paper treated with it; it is free from Chlorine and relatively non-volatile.

(2) (2) Application of Penta-chlorophenol, in a concentration of 0.1% weight of the paper. Since this is a highly chlorinated substance it has to be used either in the presence of sufficient alkali to take care of the liberation of hydrochloric acid, or in percentages less than 0.1 either in aqueous or non-aqueous solutions.

(3) Blotting paper impregnated with 1% P.C.P. is recommended to be used for interleaving with the sheets of paper as a preventive measure.

(4) Application of 0.1% non-aqueous solution of Copper Naphthenate on paper has the disadvantage of giving a slight greenish tint to the treated paper. There is also a slight risk that the presence of this chemical on paper will increase its liability to damage in a polluted atmosphere.

(5) Application of 0.1% aqueous or non-aqueous solution of Mercuric Chloride on paper is a very effective fungicide but violently

poisonous and should be used only for paper that is not handled often.

(6) Application of 0.1% aqueous or non-aqueous solution of Mercapto-Benzthiazole singly or as a mixture of this chemical in combination with Salicylanilide.

(7) According to Langwell, Salicylanilide is the mot promising fungicide for use with paper to prevent foxing. It is suggested that this chemical, in percentage mentioned above, may be used either as a solution in water or in Carbon-tetrachloride containing small amounts of acetone, to be applied or sprayed on paper.

Experiments conducted by the author to evaluate the effectiveness of Sodium salicylate showed that a concentration of 10% of the chemical in an aqueous solution is required to inhibit paper infesting fungi in India. Such a high percentage in considered detrimental to the permanence of paper and therefore cannot be recommended as effective method.

Plenderleith (1969) suggests the following methods for prevention and control of fungus growth on paper.

(1) Fumigating mould infested paper with gaseous formaldehyde. The gas is generated by adding 1 pound of aqueous formaldehyde to 6 ounces of solid potassium permanganate in porcelain basin to be used for fumigating 100 to 1500 cubic foot areas. 24 hours of fumigation is recommended.

(2) Fumigating affected paper with thymol vapour in a fumigation chamber. 1 ounce of thymol made to vapourize by using a 40 watt bulb is considered adequate for sterilizing the contents of a cupboard or chamber of 16 cubic foot capacity. Paper on which there is oil paint or varnish should not be subjected to thymol fumigation as the chemical has softening effect on them.

(3) Interleaving paper with thymolized blotting paper as a preventive measure is also recommended. Thymolized paper can be prepared by immersing bloting paper in a 10% solution of thymol in alcohol, which is dried subsequently.

(4) Protective sheets as mentioned above can also be made by impregnating paper with 10% aqueous solution of Sodium pentachlorophenate (available under the brand name 'Santobrite' in the U.K.).

Belyakova (1964) recommends the application of 1% solution of Sodium pentachlorophenate on paper to prevent fungus growth. According to this author it is non-corrosive, does not affect the mechanical strength of paper and the toxicity lasts for a long time. It is recommended that persons handling pentachlorophenate powder should be equipped with respirators or wire gauze masks over nose and mouth as it causes irritation of the mucous memberane.

Considering the fact that parts of books containing glue are the first to be attacked by moulds, several authors have recommended a number of chemical formulations for application on book covers. Wilfred Plumber (1964) gives a good compilation of the formulations used in several institutions, some of which are mentioned below:

Sri Lanka Institute of Scientific and Industrial Research

Shellac flakes	-3/4 lb
Mastic	-1/4 lb
Sandarac	-1/4 lb
Camphor	-1 oz
Alcohol	-2 litres
Olive of Lavender	- 2oz
Mercuric Chloride	- 0.7 gms

This formula is recommended for thin application on book covers, to be allowed to dry after application.

Duke Hospital Library

Ethyl Celluloe	- 10 ½ oz
Salicylanilide	- ½ oz
Xylol	- 3 ½ qt.
Butanol	- 6 oz

For application on book covers to prevent fungus growth and to keep insects away.

The National Archives, New Delhi recommends spraying of rooms with 10% Thymol in methylated spirit for general sterilization of storage areas and thymol fumigation for affected material.

The U.S. Printing Office provides the following specifications to free books from mould attack (as quoted by Wilfred Plumbe):

(i) Book cloth to be coated or impregnated with Pyroxylin or Venyl.

(ii) Nylon sewing thread to be used for stitching.

(iii) Polyvinyl acetate emulsion type resinous adhesives to be used in book binding

(iv) Book papers not to contain starch or casein.

The U.K. Crown Agents Standard Specification No. 40, 1954 recommends use of a solution containing 1% (weight in volume) of Mercuric Chloride, 0.5% beachwood creosote (volume in volume) in methylated spirit for applicationto the backs of the books before they are placed in covers, to the inside of the leather cloth and to the sides of the boards.

Short-wave ultraviolet radiation is also a recommended method of disinfection of the air and the books in libraries, archives etc.

Much of the damage to paper materials caused by fungus attack could be eliminated by adopting good 'house keeping' practices. Contol of humidity is of utmost importance. Damp and dirty walls, leakages from drain pipes, waste organic matter lying around or in nearby areas are bound to act as reservoirs of fungus infection. Paper is a hygroscopic material. It absorbs moisture from the atmosphere. Moisture not only weakens paper but promotes fungus growth. Statistics worked out by the British Museum showed that 1,000 tons of books absorbed 10 tones of water when the relative humidity of the atmosphere was increased from 57% to 63% at 60°F. To avoid absorption of atmospheric moisture by paper it should be ensured that paper, books and manuscripts are stored under proper conditions of humidity and temperature. A temperature range of 16 to 20°C and relative humidity between 45 and 55% is considered suitable for preventing fungus growth.

While treating infected books and manuscripts, care should be taken not to brush off moulds in storage areas; all affected material should be dealt within the open air.

INSECT ATTACK

The problem of insect attack on books, manuscripts and documents has been known almost from the very beginning of the use of writing materials by man. Insect damage to books is a serious problem in tropical humid countries. The most common insects that attack paper are Silver fish, Book Lice, Cockroaches, Termites, Bookworm beetles and Crickets. Some of the demisted beetles like the Furniture Carpet Beetle Carpet Beetle and Leather Beetle cause damage to the leather in book-binding. The prevention and control measures with regard to the deterioration of paper brought about by insect pests are discussed there.

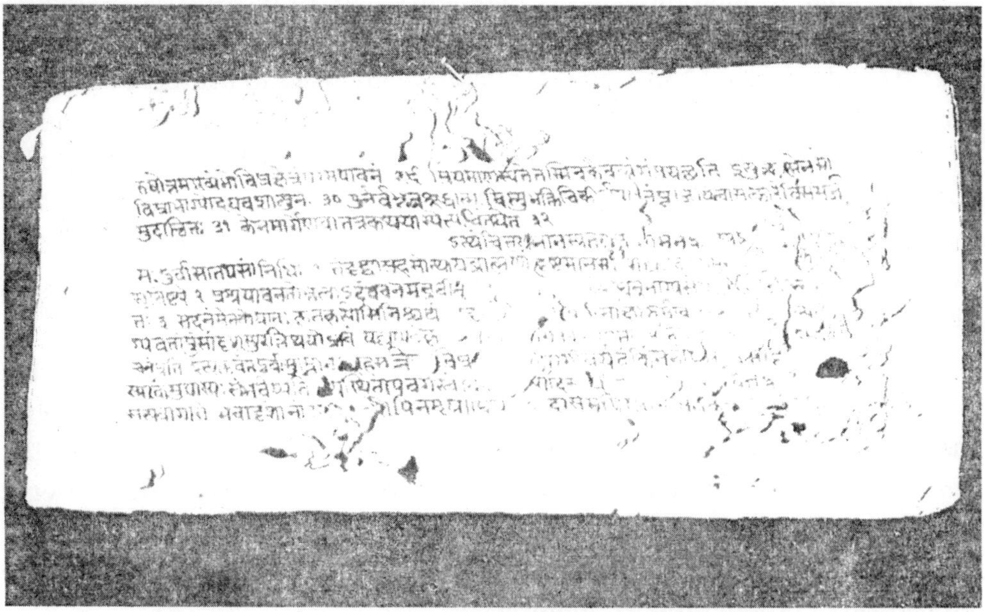

A paper manuscript attacked by sub-terranian termites.

An amazing variety of substances have been used for preventing insect attack on books from time immemorial. In the 3rd Century A.D. the Chinese invented an insecticide 'huang nieh', prepared from seeds of the Amur Cork tree *Phellodendron amurense* (Wilfred Plumbe, 1964). Smearing of books with cedar wood oil was an age old practice. Wilfred Plumber (1964) provides a compilation of the materials used over the last four centuries for protection of books and bookshelves from insect attack. These include alum, thymol, oil of anis, cajuput oil, bitter chestnuts, beeswax, bitumen, camphor, cinchona, red chillies, borax, benzene, cinnamon, cloves, clove oil, copal varnish, creosote, oil of eucalyptus, formalin, chloropicrin, lanolin, lac varnish, mercuric chloride, naphthalene, neem leaves, tobacco, paraffin wax, petroleum, phenic acid, porpoise oil, pyrethrum powder, sandalwood, oil of sassafras, shellac, snuff, turpentine etc.

In India various indigenous plant products were used as pesticides or repellents from very early times. Leaves of the Neem tree *(Azadirachta Indica)* and tobacco *(Nicotinum tabacum)* were used to protect books and manuscripts. Powdered rhizomes of Sweet flag *(Acorus calamus)*, known as 'Godavaj' in Gujarati, is being used as an insect repellent in manuscript collections of the Oriental Institute, University of Baroda, Gujarat State even today. Evidences are also available of the use of Camphor, Sandalwood oil, clove and cidrus deodara oils. Palm leaf manuscripts used to be hung above the cooking fire place in kitchens in South India.

Recent advances in the field of pesticides have made available today a wide range of insect repellent and insecticidal chemicals, and several methods and techniques of using them effectively. However, many of the pesticides available in the market and those used in agriculture and commerce are not suitable for use in museums, archives or libraries. Fortunately, a lot of information is available today about methods successfully used for the protection of bibliographical material.

Preventive measures are perhaps more important in the protection of paper, books etc. because they are aimed at avoiding insect damage to paper. This can be achieved, apart from ensuring cleanliness of the surroundings, free circulation of air and control of humidity and temperature, by using chemical repellents. Once infestation has set in, control measures will have to be resorted too.

Use of Repellents

Para-di-chlorobenzene is a repellent chemical used universally. To be effective, crystals of p.d.c.b. should be present in a quantity of 1 lb. to 1 cubic ft. of air space in an airtight cupboard (Plenderleith, 1969). Naphthalene, another repellent used for the same purpose, is less effective, than p.d.c.b. In search for an effective repellent against the common insect pest of museums in India, the author tried a large number of chemicals and chemical formulations. One of the formulae that gave satisfactory results is a mixture of p.d.c.b., Benzene and Creosote. The composition of this formulation, called p.b.c., is as follows:

Paradichlorobenzene	- 50 gms
Benzene	- 50 cc.
Creosote	- 50 cc.

Wilfred Plumbe (1964) recommends use of a mixture of Carbon tetrachloride and Ethylene oxide in cupboards, to be placed at the top shelf, the vapour being heavier than air.

Insecticidal Book Varnishes and Lacquers

Several varnishes and lacquers with the addition of suitable insecticides are used in many libraries for protection of books. As early as 1887, the Chinese were using a mixture of 5 drams of Mercuric chloride, 60 drops of creosote and 2 lbs. of alocohol for application on books covers to prevent insect damage. In Puerto Rico a varnish consisting of one litre of wood alcohol, 30 gms. of Carbolic acid and 15 gms. of Mercuric chloride was applied on books at intervals of 6 months, a practice that existed before the first World War. In Figi in 1930, a solution of one ounce of Mercuric Chloride and 1 ½ ounce of Carbolic acid in one quart of methylated spirit containing Pyridine was being employed. The Deartment of Agriculture in Ceylon (now Sri Lanka) recommended a mixture of Ammonium arsenite and Mercuric Chloride (one ounce) in a pint of rectified spirit, occasionally with the addition of beechwood creosote. Mercuric Chloride, Carbolic acid and Creosote were also used in various formulations in Cuba, Trinidad, Ghana, Nigeria, Singapore and Malaya (Wilfred Plumbe, 1964).

The Shell International Co. recommends a liquid insecticide product called 'Dieldrex 15' for app;ication on book bindings. Lacquers containing Dieldrin or Aldrin are applied on book shelves in libraries in Zanzibar, Nigeria and Malaya. The Centre National de la Researche Scientifique (CNRS),

Paris developed a wax called 'Cire-212', in 1959 which is recommended for application to leather book bindings. The British Museum, London recommends use of a formulation called British Museum Leather Dressing (BMLD) consisting of Hexane – 11 oz, anhydrous Lanolin – 7 oz, Cedarwood oil – 10 oz and beeswax ½ oz. It is primarily meant as a preservative for leather, but helps also to keep insects away.

The New York Public Library recommends another formulation as follows: Neatfoot oil – 25 oz; anhydrous Lanoolin – 12.5 oz.; Japanese Wax – 10 oz.; Sodium stearate – 2.5 oz. and distilled water 45 oz.

Use of Contact Insecticides and Fumigants

Contact insecticides are used as powders or in spray solutions. Treating the walls of cupboards and premises with 10 to 30% DDT powder or 0.5 to 2% DDT dust suspension as sprays is an effective method of insect control. It can also be used in the form of suspensions in organic solvents like Petrol, Kerosine or Turpentine. Plenderleith (1969) recommends that when insects are discovered the drawers, cupboards, shelving etc. be thoroughly cleaned and dusted with persistent insecticides such as DDT or BHC (Gammexane). Chakraborti (1949) warns against exposing papers to Gammexane smoke as it can cause a substantial decrease in the tensile strength and folding endurance as well as cause iron gall ink to fade.

Solutions containing Dieldrin, Malathion or Diazinon are also effective for area treatment. Another very useful insecticide used either as dust or spray is Pyrethrum.

As none of the above mentioned chemicals can be applied directly on paper, books, manuscripts or documents, the only effective means of dealing with such material already infested by insects is fumigation. Hydrogen Cyanide is a foolproof fumigant but it should be used only by a qualified pest control operator. Vacuum fumigation with Ethylene oxide and Carbondioxide or Methyl alos gives good results. Carbon tetrachloride alone or a mixture of this with Ethylene oxide both are used as fumigants in some libraries and museums. Paradichlorobenzene is another chemical which can be used as a fumigant as well.

Sprays or dusts containing 5% DDT, BHC or Pyrethrum, 2% Malathion, 2% Chlordane and the use of Paradichlorobenzene or PBC as repellents were found effective for the prevention and control of silver fish. Another method of controlling silver fish is by taking advantage of its craving for starchy food and poisoning it with a bait consisting of a mixture of 12 parts of Sodium fluoride to 100 parts of wheat flour. A paste made up of ½ to ¾ ounce of white Arsenic (Arseneous oxide) with 1 pint of wheat flour mixed with enough water is also a good bait. The paste should be poured on pieces of cardboard or paper which can be folded into cylinders with the paste on the inside. Dusting of Pyrethrum on book shelves or surrounding areas is useful for controlling silver fish, provided it is renewed often. Back (1931) recommends a spay solution made by saturating Paradichlorobenzene in Carbon tetrachloride for quickly killing hoards of silver fish which one may come across in storage areas. The Carbon tetrachloride evaporates and fine crystals of p.d.c.b. will form on the sprayed material which in turn soon evaporates causing no damage. Spraying an infested room with this mixture and keeping it closed for 24 hours also will eradicate silver fish. For cockroaches sprays/dusts containing 5% DDT, BHC or Pyrethrum are recommended. A mixture of Sodium fluoride and Gypsum (1:1) can be used as a poison powder. Whenever direct application of the insecticide on cockroaches is possible it is preferable to use an insecticidal spray using an organic solvent.

To control termites, termite proofing of the building is essential. Other precautions to be taken inside museums, libraries etc. involving treatment of timber work are of a general nature and discussed in a later section dealing with wooden objects. Pyrethrum sprays, p.b.c. or p.d.c.b. were found to be effective against book lice. For book-worm beetles, dermestids and crickets exposure to p.b.c. vapour, use of p.d.c.b. as a repellent and fumigation with Carbon di-sulphide, Carbon tetrachloride, Methyl Bromide etc. are recommended.

WOOD AND WOOD PRODUCTS

Wood has played a very important role in human civilization from palaeolithic times. There is hardly any other material that man has exploited for so many purposes. For wheels and weapons, furniture and houses, boats and bridges, agricultural implements, musical instruments and art work, timber was transformed into a variety of objects. In modern times it is an essential raw material for paper, packaging, clothing and so on. It is natural, therefore, that a large number of wooden objects form a significant part of museum collections. Preservation of these materials is a matter of considerable importance.

Being an organic material chiefly composed of carbohydrates in the complex form of cellulose, wood is susceptible to a wide range of biodeterioration, mainly by fungi and insects. Knowledge about the kinds of wood may be useful in understanding the food preferences of the various wood destroying organisms. It is necessary to distinguish between hard woods and soft woods as some insect pests are specific to either one. Hard wood is a general term used for timber obtained form foliageous or deciduous trees such as oak, beech, teak, walnut etc. Soft woods are timbers obtained from needle-leaved or coniferous trees such as pine and fir. All types of wood structurally show three different areas visible in a cross section. The outer covering is the bark. Inside the bark is the 'sap wood', usually light in colour, less compact and containing a large amount of moisture. This is the living part of the tree. Within the sapwood and in the centre of the tree trunk is the 'Heart wood', generally darker in colour, more compact and dense containing less moisture. This is the part of the tree that gives it strength.

Wood is made up chiefly of four items, namely, cellulose which makes up about 70% of the wood substance, lignin that accounts for 18 to 20%, minerals comprising 0.2 to 1.0% and the remainder made up of extractives such as gums, oils, resins, sugars, tannins etc. There is also a large amount of moisture present in wood.

Conditions of storage play a major role in determining the nature of biodeterioration. Wood in contact with the earth is liable to be attacked by termites, wood worms and fungi more easily. Warm and moist environments provide suitable conditions for their proliferation. Sap wood is usually more susceptible to biodeterioration compared with heart wood. Resistance to deterioration also varies with different kinds of wood. Some like teak, cedar, chestnut, walnut etc. are more resistant to decay than others.

Under certain conditions wood is one of the most durable materials. In Norway, for example, there are still functioning churches made of timber, built over 1000 years ago (Mourier and Winding, 1977). But in unfavourable conditions, timber may disappear in a few years, destroyed by insects and fungi. As a matter of fact, the nutritional content of wood is poor and only a few organisms which have special adaptations for digesting cellulose and lignin are capable of utilizing wood as food. Wood destroying bacteria and fungi produce digestive enzymes that can break down cellulose and lignin to simpler sugar compounds to be absorbed. Some wood boring beetle secrete such digestive enzymes in the stomach but, even then, wood ingested in not fully utilized. The undigested wood is ejected out in the form of faecal pellets. Some beetles like the Powder post beetle attack only those portions of wood (mainly sap wood) containing enough starch and sugar. Other insects including termites that attack timber harbour certain micro-organisms which help break down the wood for digestion.

Fungi and insects including termites constitute the most destructive organisms causing wood decay in tropical countries. Although several species attack timber in its various stages from living tree to timberyard, only a limited number are able to breed in the dry, seasoned timber that constitutes most wooden objects in museum collections.

Fungus Attack on Wood

It is largely because of its cellulosic content and hygroscopic behaviour that wood is attacked by fungi. The inception and spread of fungi on wood depends upon temperature and moisture conditions in the atmosphere. While certain kinds of mould growth cause little or no structural change, there are others capable of seriously destroying timber. The former are the ordinary filamentous fungi whereas the latter are the 'dry-rot fungi'. On the whole, an extremely large variety of fungal species grow on wooden objects.

The common filamentous fungi found to grow on wooden objects in museums in India are as follows:

1. Aspergillus niger
2. Aspergillus flavus
3. Aspergillus ochraceous
4. Fusarium clamydosporum
5. Penicillium rubrum
6. Penicillium funicolosum, Penicillium crysogenum
7. Sordaria species
8. Mucor species

The above fungi can thrive on wood only when there is a high humidity content in the atmosphere and if the wood surface has 30 to 50% and is not of great consequence unless the object is painted or is finely engraved or subjected to prolonged fungal attack.

The most serious form of fungal decay of wood is brought about by the 'dry-rot' fungi. These fungi can thrive in wood with water content as low as 20% and once the attack has started the fungus can spread to even driver timber. Following infection, this fungus develops within the wood radiating their hyphae in all directions. As decay progresses, the wood undergoes marked changes in colour, texture, density, compactness and strength. Heavily affected wood becomes darker in colour, dull of yellowish brown instead of the paler tint of sound wood. These changes are accompanied by cracking and warping due to the shortening of the fibres as evaporation of water content takes place. The wood also becomes very soft and could be cut with a knife almost like cheese. When dry the wood can easily be crushed to powder between the fingers. It now has a high water absorbing capacity from damp air which is a factor that has an important bearing on the progress of the disease itself. If put in water it rapidly absorbs water and sinks.

If a section of the dry-rot wood is carefully examined, fungus filaments can be found permeating in all directions. The most common dry-rot fungus belongs to a species called *Merulius lacrymans*. It has an outstanding capacity to tolerate high temperatures. In wood, they obtain their food from cellulose, lignin and other components. These fungi are also selective in their food preference. Some utilize lignin while others take cellulose, leaving the lignin intact. These two groups are respectively known as "white-rotters" and "brown-rotters". Dry rot fungi are capable of remaining dormant for several years when moisture content of the wood is insufficient, reviving their growth when conditions are favourable. Ideal conditions for their growth are moisture content of 20% and above of the dry weight of wood and temperature between 23°C and 30°C. They do not attack wood having high tannin content.

Another species called cellar fungus *(Conisphora cerebella)* is widely distributed in Europe, attacking wood that is definitely wet. It requires a high water content of 40 to 50% and therefore most commonly occurs in cellars or on roofs where leakage of water occurs. It does not grow when temperature is about 35°C.

Prevention and Control of Fungus Growth

The most important measure to be considered for prevention of fungus attack on wood, as in the case of paper, is to keep humidity under control. All sources of dampness should be identified and avoided. Chemical methods of preventing fungus growth consist of application of suitable fungicides. This can be done only on wood that is not painted. In certain cases objects can also be coated or impregnated with water-proofing agents such as linseed oil, wax or a water repellent silicone varnish (Plenderleith, 1969).

A large number of water soluble fungicides are recommended for treatment of wood. These include Sodium fluoride, Magnesium silicofluoride, Zinc chloride, Mercuric chloride, mixtures of Copper and Chromium salts and Sodium pentachlorophenate. Plenderleith recommends treatment of wood with an aqueous solution of Sodium fluoride (3-6 oz. dissolved in one gallon of water) or Magnesium fluoride (half a pound dissolved in one gallon of water) to protect it from fungus growth. These two fungicides are colourless and odourless – properties, considered favourable.

Several organic solvent preservatives are also used for prevention of fungus growth. These include organic solvents containing pentachlorophenol, metallic naphthanates, chloro naphthanates etc. Kuritsyna (1966) recommends a solution of Pentachlorophenol in Carbon tetrachloride or an 8% solution on N-cetyl pyridine chloride for spraying on wooden packaging material for prevention of fungus growth during shipment of museum materials.

Da Costa *et. al.* (1967), after making a toxicological evaluation of 11 presevatives for prevention of fungus attack on wood recommend Tributyltin oxide and *Creosote* as the most effective, followed by Pentachlorophenol.

According to them Lauryl Pentachlorophenol and Copper naphthanate failed to give satisfactory results.

A number of wood preservatives have been developed during the lat hundred years, most of which are for use with commercial timber. Some have been tried and successfully adapted for museum use. Most of these formulations fulfil the dual purpose of preventing fungus growth and insect attack. These will be discussed later while dealing with prevention and control of the insect pests of wooden objects.

Insect Attack on Wood

Insects inflict more damage to wood than do fungi. Nature of the damage depends upon the type of insect infestation, which varies in different parts of the world. The type of wood or the part of the wood affected also are decisive factors. The most common insect pests in museums, however, are termites, wood borers such as Furniture Beetle, Death-watch Beetle, Powder post Beetle, Bamboo Borer etc. A detailed account of the characteristics of these insects is given in Chapter II. Damage recognition and identification of species responsible are very important initial steps for the conservation of infested wooden objects. While examining wooden objects or structural timber one should look for worm holes and the expulsion of powdery or granular frass (faecal matter). If frass is seen to be falling from worm holes it is a sure indication that insect larvae are active inside. Similarly earthen galleries of termites indicate termite infestation.It is not always easy to find the wood boring beetles themselves around wooden objects undergoing infestation because the larval life is very prolonged in most cases and is inside the wood. It therefore becomes necessary to identify the culprint from visible secondary evidences such as worm holes and frass. A key to identifying the three major wood boring beetles from such evidence is given below:

Characteristic damage	*Insect species*	*Illustration*
The worm holes have a diameter of 1.5 to 2 mm. Frass is of uniform colour and feels gritty and almost cigar shaped.	Furniture *Beetle (Anobium punctatum de Geer)*	(photograph)
The worm holes have a diameter of 3.5 mm. The frass are large and lens-shaped.	Death watch Beetle *(Xestobium rufovillosum)*	(Photograph)
The worm holes have a diameter of 1.0 to 1.5 mm. Frass is very fine and feels like chalk.	Powder post Beetle *(Lyctus bruneus)*	(Photograph)

Prevention and Control

The use of preservatives to prevent biodeterioration of wood goes back to early times. The ancients used to preserve wood by rubbing essential oils extracted from certain kinds of wood. Several chemicals have been employed as preservatives for over a hundred years, particularly in the commercial use of timber. Most of these are materials that make wood distasteful to insects and toxic enough to prevent their attack. Most are effective against both insects and fungi. Surface coatings are very useful because they also provide a film that covers the rough texture and pores in wood preventing the deposition of eggs by insects in the pores. A wide variety of surface coatings are available today for protecting wooden objects and structural timber. The common commercial preservatives include creosotes, anthracene oils, petroleum, tar etc. Water soluble salts such as Zinc chloride, Mercuric chloride, sodium fluoride, Copper sulphate, Zinc meta arsenite etc. are also used. Antoher control measure is fumigation with Methyl bromide, Sulphuryl fluoride, Ethylene oxide, Hydrogen cyanide or Carbon di-sulphide. Wood can also be sterilized by impregnation with liquid insecticides.

A formulation called 'Woolman Salt' is approved for use as a wood preservative by the American Wood Preservers Association. It is reported that it is highly effective against insect attack and fungal decay. This consists of –

Sodium fluoride – 25%; Sodium hydrogen arsenate – 25%;

Sodium chromate – 7 ½% and Dinitrophenol – 12 ½%.

Plenderleith (1969) recommends the use of DDT, BHC, Pentachlorophenol, Chloronaphthalenes or metallic naphthanates as suitable insecticides. He also recommends a mixture of DDT powder in molten wax for filling up worm holes on wooden objects. Where wetting wooden objects is not of any serious consequence he recommends dipping them in a hot 4% aqueous solution of Zinc chloride or Sodium fluoride.

The Forest Research Institute, Dehra Dun (India) recommends a formulation called ASCU (containing Sodium or Postassium dichromate – 4 pts., Copper sulphate – 1 pt., Arsenic pentoxide – 1 pt., and Water – 100 pts.) for treatment of structural timber for prevention of insect and fungus attack.

Hachiro Mori (1963) advocates Ethylene oxide as the most powerful fumigant for exterminating insects from wood. As Ethylene oxide is inflammable it can be used as a mixture with Carbon di-oxide as recommended for the fumigation of textiles. As the former is soluble in water its efficacy will be reduced when fumigating wood with a high water content. In Japan a mixture of Ethylene oxide and Methyle Bromide is used successfully for extermination of insects from wood. Mori does not favour the use of Methyl Bromide liquid for direct application on wood because it leaves dark brown stains. For purposes of fumigation, the standard amount of Methyl bromide used is 35-50 gm^3 at 20-30°C for 24 hours. Truman, *et.al.* (1976) recommended 2 ½ lb per 1,000 cubic feet of Methyl bromide for fumigation purposes.

The prevention and control of termite attack on wood requires special attention. The best time to ensure protection of structural timber in buildings against subterranean termites is during construction. It is important that every effort is made to provide necessary chemical soil treatment and other termite barriers during construction. This aspect of termite proofing has been developed through research and experience and has come to stay as an important pest control practice. This being a well established specialized area of work it is not necessary to go into details of the process here. For further information the reader may refer to the publication, 'Subterranean Termites, their prevention and control in buildings', Home and Garden Bulletin No. 64, 1977 published by the United States Department of Agriculture. Based on studies conducted for treating soils in southern Mississippi for protection against termite attack Harmon Johnston *et. al.* (1971) report that Aldrin, Chlordane, Dieldrin and Heptachlor applied at various concentrations (1-2% in water) are found to be effective even after 17 to 21 years.

Some further reference may, however, be made here regarding the direct chemical treatment of wood to prevent damage by termites. The oil preservatives have long been used for protecting structural timber from insect attack. In South India coal tar is coated on wooden poles fixed to the ground or structural supports holding thatched roofs to prevent termite attack.

Other chemicals used for prevention of termite damage in various parts of the world are as follows:

Creosote oil

Sodium arsenite

Pentachlorophenol

Sodium pentachlorophenate

Copper naphthanate

DDT, BHC

Chlordane

Dieldrin

Periodic inspection of buildings for evidence of termite attack is necessary. Other general precautionary practices should include (1) removal of all wood and other debris containing cellulose from underneath and adjacent to buildings; (2) impregnation with suitable insecticides of wood piers and posts that will be driven into soil; (3) filling voids, cracks or expansion joints in concrete or masonry either with cement grout, coal tar or rubberoid bituminous sealers and (4) providing adequate drainage and ventilation. Paints and varnishes on wood also act as a useful protective coating.

Finally, it may be mentioned that there are many preservatives available in the market today under various trade names. Some may be good, containing effective toxic chemicals, but many are advertised with extravagant claims about their properties and effectiveness. It is advisable not to use in museums any formulation, the composition of which is not known.

TEXTILES

Textiles are generally made up of organic fibrous materials like cotton, linen, wool, silk etc. or modified or synthetic fibres like rayon, polyester, nylon and glass fibre. Though the fibre is the chief component of a textile, additive materials such as dyes, starches, water repellents etc. also make up part of the composition. Several physical, chemical, biological and environmental factors may be responsible for deterioration of textiles. The biological agents that cause damage are mainly fungi and insects.

Textile material in museum collection generally comprises those made from plant fibres such as cotton, linen, kapok, jute etc. or those of animal origin such as wool and silk. Plant fibres are cellulosic in nature whereas animal fibres are proteinaceous. Of the various types of textiles, wool is most susceptible to insect attack whereas vegetable fibres are more vulnerable to micro-organisms.

Attack by Fungi and Bacteria

Like other organic materials, textiles are susceptible to attack by filamentous fungi and bacteria in humid conditions. Under controlled conditions of humidity, and when air is reasonably dry, mould growth is unlikely to take place. Humid conditions, however, promote considerable damage to cellulosic fibres due to fungus growth. Fungi break down cellulose rapidly weakening the strength of the fabric. Staining or discolouration is also caused by their activity.

Many of the cellulolytic bacteria discussed while dealing with paper are capable of attacking cotton and linen textiles. But their occurrence in museums is rare as they develop only under very moist conditions. With wool and silk the problem of deterioration through microorganism is negligible unless exposed to exceptional circumstances, favourable for their growth.

In tropical humid climates the major problem of biodeterioration of cellulosic fibres is that of fungus growth. Some of the most common fungi that attack such fabrics in India are several species of *Aspergillus, Penicillium, Fusarium, Mucor* and *Trichoderma* (Nair, 1970). Hardy (1943) also mentions the above species as the chief textile mildewing fungi. Several authors have reported *Chetomium globosum* causing enormous deterioration to textile fibres. Broughton-Alcock (1919) investigating the causes of deterioration of canvas attributes most of the damage to the fungal species of *Stemphyllium*. An extensive study of fungus attack on textiles in tropical countries is that of (White *et.al.,* 1948) dealing with celluloytic activity of 453 species of fungi belonging to 45 genera. Prindle

(1935) suggests that the species of the genera *Alternaria, Stemphyllium, Oospora* and *Penicillium* are destructive to woolen fabrics.

Silks and rayons are also affected by fungi. It has been observed that synthetic fibres like nylon and polyester may show superficial growth of fungi, without impairing the strength of the fibre. Such growths are apparently the result of either impurity or soiling (Hueck, 1972)

Fungicidal Treatments

When fungus is found on textiles, the first step to be taken is to remove the growth with a soft brush. This should be followed by appropriate chemical treatment for prevention and control. Plenderleith (1969) recommends sterilization of the textile with thymol vapour to prevent further growth.

A large number of anti-mildew agents are available in the market today. But most of these are meant for agricultural applications and the problem of choosing an appropriate fungicide for textiles in museums is still a difficult one. Hueck (1972) provides a compilation of fungicides for textiles including some of the followings:

Phenyl mercuric acetate

Zinc dimethyldithiocarbamate

Copper-8-quinolinolate

Copper naphthanate

Salicylanilide

Diaphene

Pentachlorophenol

Sodium Pentachlorophenate

Triphenyltinacetate

Triphenyltinhydroxide

Formaldehyde

Para-dichlorobenzene

Ethylene oxide

The concentrations for the fungicides recommended are 0.5-1% of the weight of the fabric, except for phenylmercuric acetate and triphenyltin compounds which are to be used in lower concentrations.

Simple spraying of textile with fungicides is not always likely to give desirable results. Only impregnation of fabrics will provide adequate protection. Alcoholic sprays ensure better penetration into the fabric, thus giving longer protection. Hueck does not recommend all the fungicides listed above for use with delicate textiles. A number of them, particularly copper compounds are coloured. It is also said that phenol derivatives and compounds slowly break down when exposed to day light with undersirable effect on textiles. A weak acidic chemical such as pentachlorophenol is suspected to cause deterioration to cellulosic fibres because of its acidic reaction. Formaldehyde is known to have a hardening effect on proteinaceous materials and as such not recommended for use on woolen textiles. According to Baynes Cope (1966) it may also cause fading of blue dyes. Jedrzejewska (1967) is of the opinion that Naphthalene should not be used for woolen textiles because it promotes an alkaline reaction on wool. Lehmann (1964) rules out both Naphthalene and paradichlorobenzene for wool on account of their damaging influence. Experience of using these chemicals for protection of woolen materials in India, however, does not substantiate this view.

Based on Czerwinska's (1953) studies which have shown the use of Salicylanilide as an effective fungicide for archival materials, Hueck recommends it for cellulosic fibres. This active fungicide is colourless, odourless and non-volatile. The use of Salicylanilide in combination with quaternary ammonium compounds and with halogenated derivatives is recommended by Partridge (1949).

As a general rule, impregnation with fungicides should be considered only as a last alternative. 1% pentachlorophenol in kerosene, 5% Laurylpentachlorophenol in turpentine or alcohol or 3-5% alcoholic solution of p-chloro-m-cresol are recommended for fungicidal treatment of textiles by Hueck. Affected textiles can be disinfected by fumigation. Formaldehyde has been used by many for this purpose. It is not a suitable chemical for treating woolen textiles. Now-a-days Ethylene oxide is highly recommended for disinfection purposes (Plenderleith, 1966). In order to overcome the explosive nature of Ethylene oxide, Czerwinska *et. al.* (1956) recommend the use of this chemical in a mixture with Carbon di oxide. Rice (1962) suggests the use of a mixture of Freon and 11% Ethylene oxide. Paradichlorobenzene, the commonly used insect repellent in museums can also be used to prevent mildew. Block (1951) recommends an amount of 40 gm/m^3 of air. It is not, however, as effective as other fungicides mentioned earlier.

Most of the fungicides recommended for use with paper materials can be used for cellulosic fibres also, including fumigation processes. It must be emphasized, however that control of humidity and temperature should form the best preventive measure to safeguard textile collections.

Insect Attack

Textiles of cellulosic constitution are not generally subjected to much insect damage compared with textiles made up of animal hair. Occasional pests of cellulosic fibres include silver fish, cockroaches, crickets and termites. Even for these insects, textiles are not the first food preference. Barring termites which can destroy a wide variety of fabrics containing cellulose the others are attracted to textiles because of the presence of sizing materials such as starch, dextrine, dyes and water-repellents.

Silver fish, *Lepisma saccharina* is found to attack heavily starched cotton, linen, lace or muslin, artificial cellulose-based silk, rayon and even sized silk. The house cricket, *Acheta domesticus* may eat plant fibres, silk and wall hangings. It is known to cause cuts of various lengths in fabrics. An Australian species, *Paragryllacris combustae* is reported to damage curtains by cutting a piece from the material to form a flap under which it hides (Szent Ivani, 1968). Cockroaches attack soiled and old textiles.

Fabrics made of animal hair, namely wool, attract a large number of insects which have a remarkable capacity to feed on and digest keratin of which hair is made up. Keratin is a protein which is quite stable chemically and very resistant to most means of digestion. Only a relatively small number of insects are able to digest it. The peculiar ability of these insects for keratin digestion, coupled with the widespread use of wool and other animal hair for textiles, carpet etc. poses a major pest control problem for museums. Studies conducted on museum pests in India show that certain species of clothes moths and dermestid beetles are the major pests of woolen fabrics. The most important species among them are Clothes moths and Carpet beetles.

Among the clothes moths that damage woolen fabrics in museums in India, it was observe that the most common pest is the Case-bearing Clothes Moth, less commonly found in India but more predominent in Europe and North America is the Webbing Clothes Moth, *Tineola bisselliella.* The moth is almost the same in size as the Case-bearing Clothes Moth, but buff-coloured with silvery brown wings without spots. The larvae are shiny, creamy white and spin silken threads making random patches under which they confine their feeding activity. They form webs rather than making a case around them. Another Clothes Moth worth mentioning is the Tapestry Moth, *Trichophaga tapetzella.* This is the largest moth that attacks textiles and the larvae have a preference for coarser materials including old woolen blankets, horse hair, furs and feathers. The larva makes a silk tube or burrow through the material on which it feeds.

Dermestid beetles are known for devastating attacks on wool, leather and mounted animal specimens in museums. Among those attacking

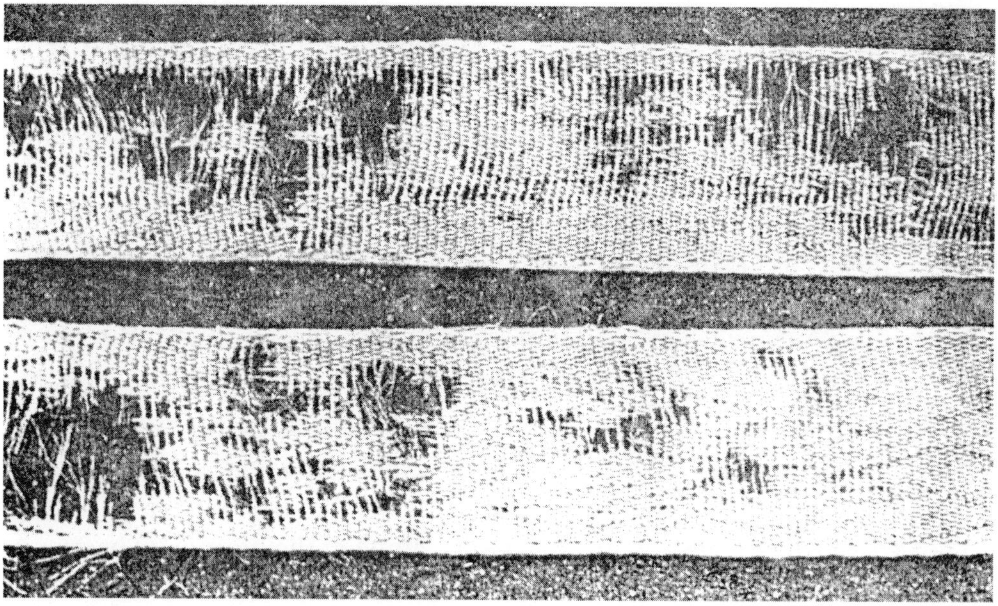

Artificial silk ribbon damaged by silver fish (Courtesy, Collin's Guide to Wild Life in House and Home.

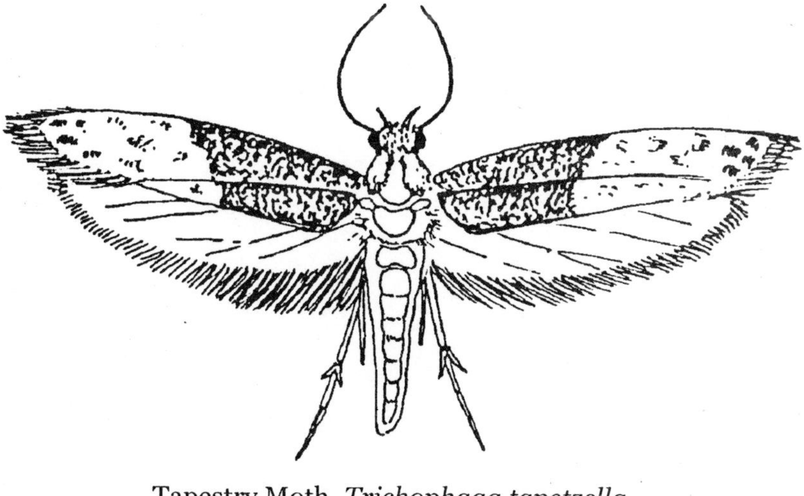

Tapestry Moth, *Trichophaga tapetzella.*

woolen fabrics two species are most conspicuous as museum pests in India. These are Furniture-Carpet beetle, *Anthrenus flavipes* and the Carpet Beetle, *Attagenus gloriosae.*

Another species of Carpet Beetle found in India, closely resembling *Attagenus gloriosae* is the Black Carpet Beetle, *Attagenus piceus.* It is often difficult to distinguish between the larvae of these two species, but the adult appearance is distinctive, the Black Carpet Beetle having a uniformly black colour without the transverse band present in the other. Of the two *Attagenus gloriosae* is more commonly found in museums in India.

Compared to wool, silk is a more stable material from the point of view of biodeterioration. Silk is a lustrous fibre produced by the larvae of silk worms. It consists of a substance known as fibroin which is held together by a silk gum called sericin. Though 95% of the silk fibre consists of protein it has very little nutritive value for insects. None of the dermestid beetles or carpet beetles are known to be able to survive on silk. Sizes and stains may attract some insects to silk. Some of the fabric pests are known to have a special affinity for stains on textiles due to urine, sweat, blood, fruit juices, milk, coffee and other food stains (Mallis *et. al.,* 1959).

Prevention and Control of Insect Attack

Prevention and control of fabric pest infestation require a thorough knowledge of the biology and habits of the insects concerned and careful workmanship.

Preventive Measures

Preventive measures must be the key to pest control. These include good 'house-keeping' practices and actual protection by chemical measures. Much can be done to prevent insect infestation through frequent cleaning with a vacuum cleaner, brushing, airing and dry cleaning whenever possible.

Prolonged, undisturbed storing should be avoided. It is also essential to avoid breeding places such as rubbish dumps containing pieces of woolen, cut off pieces of carpeting, feather etc.

Use of insect repellents in an important measure in storage areas. The most common and effective repellent is paradichlorobenzene. Woollens stored should be interspaced with crystals of this chemical avoiding direct contact on the fabric. Naphthalene is less effective than p.d.c.b. Fur storage in cold vaults is a worthwhile preventive measure. Spraying of storage cabinets (non-fabric areas) with insecticides is also a good preventive measure.

Control Measures

Control measures comprise of getting ride of infestation that has already taken place. It consists of thoroughly evaluating the infestation, instituting sanitation measures discussed above and then applying chemicals where needed. Insecticides most suitable for the control of various fabric pests are discussed below:

Silver Fish

Silver fishes are not very difficult to control. By taking advantage of their craving for starchy food they can be poisoned by using a powder consisting of a mixture of 12 parts of Sodium fluoride and 100 parts of wheat flour or with a thin paste made by mixing white arsenic, wheat flour and water. The bait should be placed in the storage area.

Dusts of 5% Chlordane, 1% dieldrin or sprays of 5% DDT, 2% Malathion, 2% Chlordane, 0.5% dieldrin in deodourized kerosene are suitable to destroy silver fishes. Pyrethrum dusted in storage areas is effective. For quickly killing hoardes of silver fishes running around, spraying with a saturated solution of paradichloroherzene in carbon tetrachloride can be recommended. As the carbon tetra chloride evaporates, fine crystals of p.d.c.b. will form on the sprayed surface but this in turn will vapourize soon, causing no damage.

Cockroaches

Most cockroaches are resistant to chlordane and dieldrin. Diazinon and malathion are more effective. Boric acid, pyrethrum aerosol, pyrethrum or Baygon sprays used in combination with Boric acid quickly kills cockroaches. Any organic solvent based spray is far more effective because of the dissolving effect of the solvent on the wax content of the cuticle and wings of the cockroach.

Crickets

Sprays of 1% Baygon, 1% Diazinon, 2% Malathion are good insecticides for killing crickets. Baygon (2%) bait is also useful.

Clothes Moths

Clothes Moths can easily be controlled by exposing infested textiles to paradichlorobenzene with a vapour concentration of 3 m.g. per litre of air. Sprays of p.d.c.b in carbon tetrachlorids, 0.5% Diazinon and 2% Pyrethrum are also recommended.

Carpet Beetles

Carpet beetles are very resistant to most of the repellent chemicals normally used in museusms. Fumigation of the infested material with Methyl Bromide, Carbon di-sulphide or carbon tetrachloride would be effective to destroy existing infestation. Pyrethrum sprays are quite effective. Chloradane, DDT and Malthion are also used as sprays.

Textile material heavily infested by insects may be fumigated periodically with suitable fumigants such as Carbon di-sulphide, Carbon tetrachloride, Methyl Bromide etc. Woolen textiles in closets may be protected by spraying closet walls and baseboards with 5% DDT as a general precautionary measure. The use of tightly sealed plastic containers as barriers is known to prevent attacks by larvae of carpet beetles and clothes moths.

Formalin and paradichlorobenzene are effective fumigants against the clothes moth. But both are ineffective against carpet beetle larvae. Sprays of 2% chlordane, recommended by the United States Department of Agriculture is found effective in killing relatively resistant carpet beetle larvae.

An excellent paper by Hueck (1972) on 'Textile pests and their control', issued as Communication No. 449 of the Central Laboratorium, TNO, Delft, the Netherlands summarises the recommendations for controlling textile pests as follows:

1. Good housekeeping, regular inspection and vigilance provide a sound basis for the control of undesirable insect pests and micro-organisms in collections of textiles.
2. If possible, the atmosphere in textile museums should be conditioned at 50% relative humidity in order to prevent development of mildew.
3. If air-conditioning is impracticable, a relative humidity between 50% and 65% should be achieved, if possible, by manipulating ventilation and heating. Rapid fluctuations or uneven distribution of temperature should be avoided.
4. Constant storage of textiles below temperatures of 10°C (preferably 5°C) will prevent damage by insects.

5. Insecticides and fungicides should be used preventatively only, if other methods of prevention fail. If organisms are already present, these compounds should be used after checking their compatibility with the textiles concerned.
6. For preventive purposes with respect to insects contact insecticides (D.D.T., Lindane, etc.) may be used, preferably applied as a spray on walls, floors, ceilings, etc.
7. For protection against mildew, salicylanilide or quaternary ammonium compounds are suggested tentatively. In each case, proper care should be taken to investigate compatibility with the textile to be treated.
8. For curative control of both insects and micro-organisms, commercially available mixtures of ethylene oxide and inert gases may be used.

LEATHER OBJECTS

Animal skin and skin products have been used by man for a variety of purposes from time immemorial. Animal skins have served as water-carriers, sails, tents, domestic utensils, hunting gear and clothing. Untreated skins were not durable being liable to attack by micro-organisms, fungi and insects. With the advent of the process of tanning, leather came into existence; tanning strengthened and reinforced the skin. The process evolved from the primitive method of curing by smoking and oiling into advanced processes of vegetable, mineral or oil tanning. This ensured prevention of putrefaction. In the making of leather the dermal layer of the skin is used after removing the hair and epidermal layers in the process of tanning. Leather, therefore, is a collagenous complex in combination with the tanning materials.

Today leather occupies a position of significance of utilitarian as well as artistic importance. Museum collections include many leather objects and skin products of ethnographical importance. Manuscripts written on leather, parchment or vellum also form part of cultural property. Because of their protein content they are susceptible to attack by insects. Mould growth is also a common problem in humid environments. Opinions differ as to whether or not fungi can digest collagen and thus actually cause destruction of leather. Whether any significant deterioration is caused through fungus attack or not, it can make the surface of a leather object unsightly and necessitate frequent cleaning.

Fungus Attack

Mildewing of leather book bindings, shoes, hand bags etc. in humid atmospheres, particularly during the monsoon season is a common phenomenon. Identification of fungi growing on such objects show that the common leather infesting fungi in India are *Aspergillus* niger, *Aspergillus flavus, Cladosporium* species, *Penicillium* species and *Pullularia pullulans.* Many of the other paper infesting species of fungi are also found on leather.

In the prevention of fungus growth, control of humidity is the most important step. Relative humidity above 65% promotes germination of fungus spores. Vegetable and oil tanned leather is more prone to mould growth than chrome tanned leather. The latter is safe because of the presence of chromic oxide which acts as a fungicide.

For the prevention of mould growth on leather objects, Plenderleith (1969) recommends the use of an aqueous or alcoholic solution of .35% Paranitrophenol or 0.25% Pentachlorophenol. The National Bureau of Standards, USA (1948) suggests the use of a mixture of the above two fungicides at 0.2%. Higher concentrations of Paranitrophenol are not advisable because of the yellow stain caused on the object. A sodium salt of Pentachlorophenol (available in the trade name "Santobrite" in the U.K.) made into a 2% aqueous or alcoholic solution, or a lauryl derivatie known as

'Mystox L.P.-2' in a paraffin solution, are also recommended as fungicides for surface application or impregnation of leather objects (Plenderleith, 1969).

Insect Attack

Skin products are susceptible to insect attack, particularly by dermestid beetles. Though most of the common dermestids like Carpet Beetles and Furniture Carpet Beetles can cause some damage to leather the main pest is leather Beetle or Hide Beetle. The characteristics of this insect have been described in Chapter II. The larvae of the Leather Beetle, *Dermestes vulpinus* prefer untanned hides rather than leather. It is therefore a major pest of tanneries and warehouses where cured skins are stored prior to tanning. As far as leather is concerned the vegetable and oil tanned variety, parchment and vellum are more susceptible to attack by the beetle larvae. They are also attracted to mounted specimens of animals and birds in natural history collections where they feed on inadequately cured skin leaving the hair and feathers unaffected. Other insect pests of leather recorded in different parts of the world include the Varied Carpet Beetle, the Black Carpet Beetle, the Larder beetle and Spider Beetles.

Control of insects attacking skin products call for the use of suitable insecticides in the form of applications, sprays or by the process of fumigation or using repellent chemicals. Most of the repellent chemicals recommended for protecting woolen textiles, discussed earlier in this chapter, can be employed in the storage of skin products with equal success. The protection of ornithological and mammal collections in museums from dermestid beetles has been discussed in Chapter V.

Plenderleith (1969) recommends a Pyrethrum/DDT spray solution for prevention of insect attack. The solution is prepared by dissolving one ounce of Pyrethrum concentrate and one ounce of DDT in one pint of paraffin distillate. Alternatively Lethane spray solution prepared by dissolving one ounce of Lethane in 1 ½ pounds of the above mentioned distillate. In the case of heavily infested material fumigation with Hydrogen cyanide, Methyl Bromide or Carbon di-sulphide is the most effective means of control.

ETHNOGRAPHICAL COLLECTIONS

Ethnographical collections generally comprise various kind of materials used by tribal people ranging from full size dwellings reconstructed in or transferred to the museum to various utilitratian and decorative objects. Clothings, head-dresses, ornaments, ritualistic objects, water carriers, hunting gears, musical instruments, utensils and even food items form part of such collections. These may consist of wood, leather, fur, feather, wool, fibres, leaves, sticks, bamboo, horn, shell, pottery etc. used for various purposes. The dance head-dresses of many tribes are decorated with peacock feathers. Bamboo is used for building huts by some primitive tribes in South India, for making house-hold utensils, bows and arrows, fire making implements, digging sticks and musical instruments. Objects made of bark and bark fibre are used by many hill tribes as ornaments, utensils, and wearing apparel. Articles made of leaves are also used by many tribal people as aprons, mats, screens etc.

These and many other similar types of objects in the museum require adequate protection from being deteriorated by biological agencies. Organisms that attack such collections generally comprise insects, fungi and bacteria. The more easily attacked of such materials are those containing hair, feather, fur and animal skin. Many of the insects associated with such objects are almost the same as found destructive to dry preserved zoological collections in museums. Pests shun light, hide un-noticed and unless the characteristics of these insects and their damage are understood, even their presence many not be recognized by the unsuspecting custodian of the collections. It is therefore, necessary for those in charge of ethnographical materials to be conversant with the problems of biological destruction to their valuable collections.

The types of fungi that attack ethnographic collections depend upon the material. The species described for paper, wood, leather and textiles earlier in this chapter can all grow on comparable objects in ethnographical collections and it is not considered necessary to repeat this information here.

Based on a study conducted at the Australian Museum, Sydney, on the isolation and identification of fungi from ethonographic artifacts, Casey (1982) provides useful information on the species found. Several ethnographic artifacts from Papua New Guinea consisting of food dishes, drums, headrests, axes, picks, shields, netted bags, mats objects made of cain, bark, string, bamboo, musical instruments etc. were subjected to the study. Several species of *Aspergillus* and *Penicillium* were isolated and identified. These include *Aspergillus versicolour, A. restrictus, A. penicilloides, A. sydowi, A. fumigatus, Penicillium chrysognenum, P. decumbens, P. corylophilum, P. spinulosum, P. crustosum, P. citrinum, P. viridicatum, and P. puberulum*. Other fungal species found were *Wallemia sebi, Eurotium repens* and *E. rubber*. Among the species of *Aspergillus* described by Casey, the absence of *A. niger* which is the most predominent species inhabiting museum objects, is worth noting.

For control of fungus attack on ethonographical collections the methods and techniques described earlier with reference to paper, wood, textiles etc. are to be employed depending upon the type of infested material.

Insect pests that attack ethnographic material belong either to those feeding on protein substances or cellulosic materials. The major pests of animal materials are the Furniture-Carpet Beetle *(Anthrenus flavipes L.)* the Hide (Leather) Beetle *(Dermestes vulpinus* Fabricius), the Carpet Beetle *(Attagenus gloriosae* Fabricius) and the Case-bearing Clothes Moth *(Tinea pellionella L.)*. Those affecting cellulosic material are Termites, Wood-boring beetles such as the Furniture Beetle *Anobium punctatum),* the Death Watch Beetle *(Xestobium rufovillosum),* the Powderpost Beetles

(Lyctus brunneus) and the Bamboo Borer *(Dinoderus minutus)*. Others of minor significance are Book Lice *(Lipocellis* species), Silver Fish etc.

Prevention and Control

Infestation of ethonographical collections may occur within the museum or from outside at the source of acquisition of the objects. It is therefore necessary to disinfest all newly acquired collections by fumigation. In the Field Museum of Natural History, Chicago, U.S.A. a mixture of Ethylene di Chloride and Carbon tetrachloride is used to fumigate all incoming anthropological collections. Fumigation with Carbon di Sulphide or Methyl Bromide also gives good results.

Objects of basketry, wood, leather etc. may be protected by giving suitable surface coatings. Polyvinyl acetate, wax or shellac can be used for basketry, wood, bark etc. and a suitable leather dressing containing lanolin and bees wax for leather objects. It is also possible to poison some of the materials by coating with weak solutions of Sodium arsenite or Mercuric Chloride.

Another important measure that should be undertaken in all seriousness is the use of chemical repellents in storage areas. Chemicals like Paradichlorobenzene or Naphthalene in sufficient vapour concentrations my be provided in storage boxes or cub-boards. Certain chemical formulations like C.C.N. (Chloroform Creosote Naphthalein) or P.B.C (Paradichlorobenzene Benzene Creosote) if strategically placed will give even better results. These chemicals and formulations on account of their odour keep the insects away.

Treatment with Creosote, Zinc Chloride, Sodium fluoride, DDT, Chlordane or Pentachlorophenol are useful for the prevention and control of termite attack on ethnographical collections. Objects of wood, basketry etc. may also be treated with ASCU, a formulation recommended by the Forest Research Institute, Dehradun which consists of Sodium or Potassium dichromate, Copper sulphate, Arsenic pentoxide and water, if the objects do not have a painted surface.

Wood-boring beetles can be exterminated by spraying 5% pentachlorophenol in Petroleum oil or by a mixture of DDT and Pyrethrum in Kerosine. If worm holes exist the chemical may be injected into them. In serious cases of attack, fumigation with Methyl Bromide, Carbon disulphide or Hydrogen Cyanide may be done under expert supervision.

Dermestid beetles are best prevented by using PBC or CCN as repellents or in case of existing attack by fumigation with the above mentioned fumigants. Use of Pyrethrum sprays, Paradichlorobenzene, CCN or PBC is helpful in preventing attack by book lice. In the case of Clothes Moth attack the objects may be exposed to the vapour of Paradichlorobenzene or PBC or may be subjected to Pyrethrum-DDT spray.

Apart from the use of repellents, proper ventilation, periodical checking and control of temperature and humidity in the museum may go a long way in preventing biodeterioration of collections. Temperature between 20 and 25 degrees centigrade and relative humidity between 40 and 60% are ideal for the maintenance and preservation of ethnographical collections in museums.

HISTORICAL MONUMENTS AND STONE OBJECTS

Historical monuments represent the rich cultural heritage of a country. These are in the form of forts and fortresses, monuments constructed by bygone dynasties, temples, churches and mosques of archaeological importance. The preservation of such cultural property is a task of prime importance. Being exposed to the atmosphere, the climatic, physical, chemical and biological factors of deterioration continuously act upon them. In tropical humid climate the biological factors of deterioration are more predominant than in the temperate regions of the world. Biodeterioration of monuments is brought about mainly by a variety of plant growth on the stone surface. These include algae, lichens, liver-worts, mosses, ferns and even higher plants.

Cryptogamic plants such as lichens, liverworts and moss are seen to grow on almost all monuments in India. These vegetative growths have remarkable abilities to resist extreme of temperature and drought. Of these, lichens are the most deleterious to the substratum on which they grow. They are adapted to fix themselves and grow on rocks which offer no nutrition or support to other groups of plants.

There are about 16,000 different species of lichens distributed throughout the world. They can survive extremes of heat, cold, wetness and dryness. One of the remarkable features of lichens is that it is not a single plant, but is made up of an alga and a fungus living together in an intimate symbiotic relationships. Both are dependent on each another. The fungus provides shade, shelter and moisture for the alga while the alga, which possesses chlorophyll, manufactures food for itself and the fungus.

Lichens can be grouped under three categories based on the characteristics of their vegetative growth - 1) Crustose, which are found encrusted on rock or wood, 2) Fruticose, shrub like branched forms, 3) Foliose, membranous or leaf like. All these varieties can grow on rock surfaces and could be found habited on old buildings or monuments. Of these the crustose type is more common and deleterious to monuments in India. These crustose lichens appear as pale, bluish green circularly spreading patches with dark dots here and there. When in isolated patches they disfigure monuments by their contrasting colours and when in profuse growth obscure the finer details of sculptural work or carving on the rock surface.

Of the lichens that grow on rock surfaces some species prefer calcarious rocks while others like silicious rocks. These are respectively known as 'calcicolous' and 'silicolous' lichens. In some calcicolous lichens the vegetative part of the fungus is completely hidden in the stone. These are therefore known as 'endolithic' lichens. Another variety of calcicolous

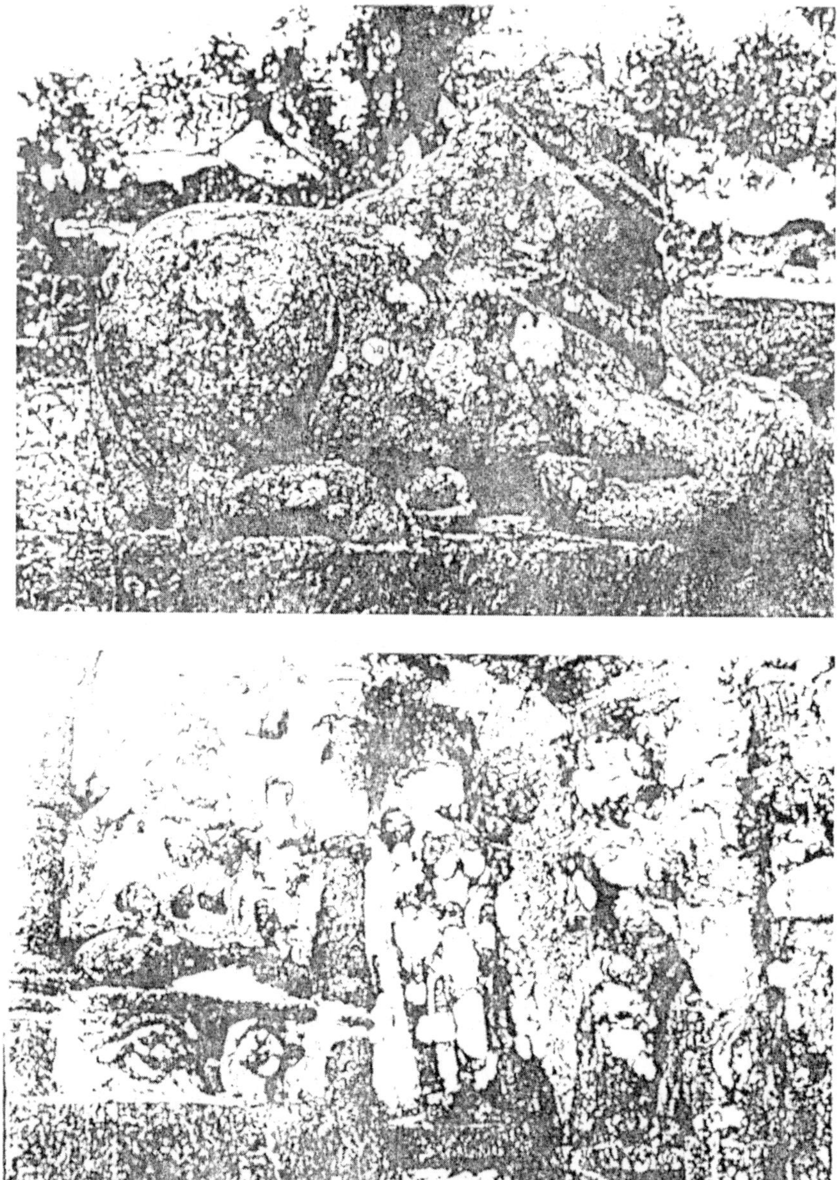

White patches on stone sculptures (in open air) brought about by the growth of crustose lichens.

lichens are the 'epithilic' lichens in which only the rhizoids, the delicate root like structures penetrate the stone. There are a few calcicolous lichens which are partially epithilic and partially endolithic. The epithilic forms are clearly visible as they are on the surface. Most of the endolithic forms are also visible to the naked eye because their fruiting bodies appear at the surface on attaining maturity. They very often give a tinge or colour to the rock surface.

The silicolous lichens are purely epilithic. The rhizoids of the endolithic, calcicolous lichens not only help in securing the plant firmly to the rock, but also servs to nourish the lichen at the expense of the stone. The rhizoids of the silicolous lichens generally perform only the function of securing the thallus to the stone.

Some are of the opinion that the presence of lichens on rock surfaces in monuments have a protective influence. But considering the function of lichens in nature as soil formers breaking down stone, it is hardly feasible that they can be protective. Even if no chemical or mechanical disintegration is brought about, the fact that they hold moisture in constant contact with the stone is to be regarded as undesirable for the protection of stone.

Algae, liverworts and moss prefer comparatively more moist surfaces than that are suitable for lichens. The liverworts derive their popular name from the superficial resemblance of their thalli (leaflike structure) to liver lobes. Moss plants grow on damp walls, in large tufts consisting of minute plants in dense crowds. The upper part of the stem bears a cluster of bright green leaf like structures.

Whereas algae, liverworts and mosses bring about comparatively minor deterioration on stone surface, lichens are known to cause deleterious effects. Patchy discolourations and eventual loss of the surface layer of stone are the result of lichen growth. Lichens are also reported to be found on frescoes exposed to open air on which they make varied alterations (Antonio Tonolo *et. al.,* 1963) Crustose lichens mar the picture surface, disfigure it and make it even unrecognizable.

Fungus attack should not normally be a problem for monuments and stone objects because they do not have any favourable nutritional substratum. However, sometimes fungus growth on frescoes are noticed. Investigations undertaken in this field by Tonolo and Giacobini (1963), Giacobini (1967), Kuritina (1968) and Savulescu and lonita (1971) led to evidences of fungal activity causing deteriorations varying from superficial spots to profound transformation of the structure of the substratum in frescoes. The growth of fungi here can be attributed to the presence of small quantities or organic substances from extraneous sources, coupled with high moisture content (Hueck, 1968).

The control of vegetative growth on monuments is not an easy task because chemical applications cannot have a lasting effect due to exposure to the atmosphere. The usual practice is that of mechanical removal of the vegetative parts followed by application of a sterilizing agent such as Zinc chloride, Zinc silico fluoride, formalin, Ammonia etc. Usually a 5% solution of any of the above may suffice. The effect of these chemicals may last only a few months, calling for repetition of the treatment. Unfortunately no dependable chemical treatment for the prevention of lichen on stone surfaces is available.

Keen (1971) recommend for the control of algae and other growths on concrete surfaces, the application of 2% formalin, 1% Dichlorophene in Alcohol, 2% Sodium pentachlorophenate or 2.5% Orthophenyl phenate. If Magnesium or Zinc silicofluorides used, 5 to 25% as required for satisfactory results according to him.

Problems of insect attack have been noticed in the famous wall paintings of Ajanta caves at Aurangabad in India. The paintings here were done on mud plaster with staraw, paddy husk and seeds of grasses used as reinforcing material. This organic content of the plaster makes it vulnerable to insect attack. A large number of irregularly shaped holes found on the painted surface are made by silver fish infestation. Many of these holes are interconnected from inside. Silver fish feed on the organic material contained in the plaster. The Spider Beetle, *Gibbium psylloides* was also found to occur. Some disfigurement was also caused by mud wasps and paper wasps which make their nests on the wall surface. Evidences of past termite attack are also noticeable on certain areas.

Conservation of wall paintings infested by insects within the plaster present a formidable problem. One of the methods recommended by the author for exterminating silver fishes and consolidating the plaster riddled by them is (i) to inject 15 to 20% formalin through the holes to force the insects out of the cavities and (ii) to fill the cavities with plaster of Paris mixed with arsenic oxide, Pyrethrum or DDT (5% weight of the plaster of Paris). Formalin is not likely to affect the painted surface as the colours used at Ajanta are mostly mineral pigments. It also has a preservative effect on the organic content of the mud plaster and will act, in addition, as a consolidate of the glue that is reported to be used as a binding medium. The incorporation of insecticides suggested above in the filler will prevent further attack by insects.

OIL PAINTINGS

Oil Paintings are those done on canvas or wooden panel in the medium of tempera or oil. They are vulnerable to biodeterioration because of the presence of the organic binding medium. when exposed to humidity, damage due to fungus attack is not uncommon. Fungi may develop on the surface of the painting, penetrating through micropores, fissures and cracks. they survive on the organic components of the binding medium and of pigments or on organic dirt that may have accumulated on the surface. Fungi may also develop on the wood or canvas support under humid conditions. Canvas that has been sized with a glue adhesive is highly susceptible to mould growth. All species of fungi that attack wood and textiles discussed earlier in this chapter may be referred to in this context.

Fungi may be mechanically removed with soft pads of cottonwool and then moistened with 10% formalin for sterilization. Plenderleith (1969) recommends the use of a non-volatile fungicide such as sodium pentachlorophenate, 2% in alcohol for prevention of further fungus growth. Fungicides recommended for textiles and wood earlier in this chapter are good for treatment of the support side of the paintings.

Wooden panels are susceptible to a wide range of insect attack under favourable conditions. Termites and wood-boring beetles have already been discussed earlier. The painted surface of the panel generally acts as a protective layer preventing insect attack from that side, but the unpainted side of the support is quite vulnerable. Worm holes found on the panel may be filled with a mixture of wax and pyrethrum. While using an insecticide for general treatment it has to be ensured that the chemical will not damage either paint or varnish. According to plenderleith the most satisfactory form of treatment is fumigation with carbon di sulphide.

METALS

The fact that microorganisms can play a role in the corrosion of metals was indicated by J.H. Garret as early as 1891. In discussing the increase in the corrosive action of water on lead caused by compounds of nitrogen, he suggested that the ammonia content of water might be increased through the bacterial breakdown of ammonia to nitrite or nitrate, thereby making the water more corrosive. In the microbial, corrosion of iron, Gaines (1910) showed the role of sulphur reducing bacteria, sulphur oxidizing bacteria and iron bacteria. Ellis (1919) and Harder (1919) reported the formation of deposits in water pipes by iron bacteria. One of the most important contributions to the field is the studies conducted by Wolzogen kuhr and Van der vlugt (1934) which showed that anaerobic bacteria of the genus *Desulfovibrio* causes corrosion by a cathodic depolarization mechanism. Most of the information available on microbial corrosion of metals is focused in the mechanism of corrosion of iron and steel in neutral anaerobic environments. Some recent studies by Churchill (1963) and Ward (1963) show the corrosion of aluminum alloys in aerobic and anaerobic environments such as the severe corrosion of these alloys in contact with hydrocarbon fuels, particulary in the wings of jet aircrafts. Very recently Inove and Takao (1982) reported the presence of 32 species of bacteria and three species of fungi causing corrosion of alluminimum alloy in aircraft. One of the most comprehensive accounts available on the mechanism of microbial corrosion is of Iverson (1976).

The above refernces on the subject have been cited here to enable interested readers to explore further on the subject of microbial corrosion of metals. In museum collections, however, corrosion of metals through microorganisms does not take place as it can generally happen only in aqueous environments in the presence of organic matter.

GLASS

Certain species of fungi can grow on damp glass sufaces in the presence of organic material. Fungi do not, however, grow on clean glass. Dust, grease and insect excrements or other organic matter are the contaminants that promote mould growth.

Under tropical climatic conditions, biological growths on optical components of cameras, projectors etc. and microscopic slides in storage present a serious problem. Even small developments of mould on optical components will lower the quality of light emission. Most often fungus growth is accompanied by corrosion of glass. When fungus grows on glass under moist condition, liquid films form around the hyphae and in many cases, deterioration of the surface of the glass by oily drops or etching in the form of indentations produced by organic acids and other chemical substances liberated by the growth processes of fungi is observed (Razumovskaya and Mitushova, 1957). According to these authors, the common fungi that can grow on glass are *Aspergillus versicoler, A. glaueus, penicillum glaucum, P. chrisogenum, Cladosproim sp., Trichoderma sp., Alternaria sp., Mucor, Aspergllus niger and Chaetomium globossum.*

For the prevention of fungus growth on glass, desiccation and application of fungicides are rcommended. Sodium methoxiethyl-mercury acetate and Methylene thiocyanate are considered suitable. According to Sviriodova and Syikovskaya (1957) the glass should be washed in spirit, dried and then placed in 0.25% solution of methoxiethyl mercury acetate in ethyl alcohol for 10 to 20 hours at room temperature. It is then to be taken out and dried. Dayal, Dixit and Agrawal (1970) recommend the wrapping of slides, optical glasses etc. in a volatile fungicidal and insecticidal paper developed by the Defence Research Laboratory. Kanpur (India) for prevention of fungus growth.

Shirk (1954) recommends the use of a volatile liquid chemical, m-cresol acetate incorporated in an ethyl cellulose base, commercially available under the name "cresatun" in the U.S.A. for application in the inner walls of optical instruments and cameras to inhibit fungus growth.

Materials like plastics, rubber etc. which were believed to be safe against microorganisms may also suffer biodeterioration under exceptional circumstances. A reference may be made of an excellent account on 'regeneration of plastics by microorganisms' by Mayumi Inove (1972) dealing with the subject in considerable details.

Chapter V

BIODETERIORATION OF NATURAL HISTORY SPECIMENS - CAUSES AND CONTROL

Collections and exhibits in a natural history museum comprise mostly of plant and animal material prepared and preserved in various ways. Some specimens are mounted in liquid preservatives containing alcohol or formalin, while others are prepared as dry specimens. The latter include dry-preserved invertebrate animals such as sponges, corals, star fishes and insects; vertebrates like reptiles, birds and mammals, herbarium collections, dried cereals, nuts and other plant products.

Apart from actual specimens, the exhibits in a natural history museum include models of plants and animals done in different media such as wax, plaster of Paris, latex, paper, mache, fiberglass and synthetic resins. In recreating natural habitats in the form of dioramas, mounted specimens, models, dried foliage and twigs along with other materials are used. The conservation of such collections and exhibits therefore is a complex problem involving a variety of substances of diverse composition. This chapter, however will deal only with the problems of biodeterioration of plant and animal materials which are susceptible to fungal and insect attack. For the sake of convenience these are dealt with under two categories, namely, botanical specimens and zoological specimens.

BOTANICAL SPECIMENS

Collections of plant specimens are generally preserved either as wet mounts using different chemical formulations in which alcohol and formalin are the essential preservatives, or as dry mounts, in the form of herbarium specimens. Biodeterioration is not a problem with regard to wet preserved specimens as they are immersed in a preservative liquid which does not allow deterioration to take place. Herbarium collections being dried plant material are susceptible to biological attack, particularly by fungi and insects. Other dry preserved plant products such as wood samples, cereals, nuts etc. are also susceptible.

Fungus Growth

In the process of preparing herbarium collections one of the stages is to make specimens 'poisonous' and thereby useless for fungi and insects to thrive upon. A successful method of doing this, one practiced by plant collectors for a long time, is the dipping of specimens in an alcoholic solution of 1% Mercuric chloride or applying it on the specimen. Being a highly corrosive and poisonous substance, extreme care has to be exercised while using it. There are other chemicals recently introduced to substitute Mercuric chloride. The British Museum Herbarium instituted a procedure using an organic compound, namely, lauryl pentachlorophenate. Sir George Taylor (1962) recommends a 3.75% solution of this chemical used in white spirit (pure white kerosene free from paraffins). It is harmless to man and does not affect clothing or paper adversely. It is claimed that this solution prevents fungus as well as insect attack.

No chemical treatment of the above nature can, however, give a lasting fungicidal effect to such collections. Fungus growth on dried herbarium plants is a common problem in tropical countries in the presence of high humidity. It has been observed that most of the cellulose decomposing fungi can attack herbarium collections. In India several species of *Aspergillus, Fusarium* and *Pencillium* and most of the other paper infesting fungi grow on herbarium collections under favourable conditions.

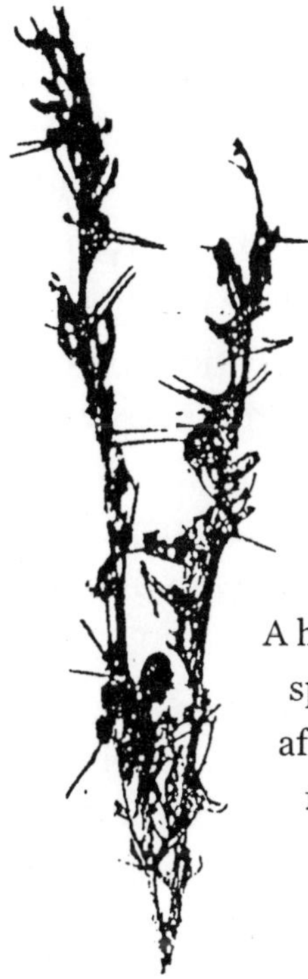

A herbarium specimen affected by fungus.

Controlling the relative humidity in storage areas is the most important step in preventing fungus growth. If the relative humidity is maintained between 45 and 55% much of the damage by fungi can be prevented. Use of fungus repellants should also be considered. Most of the fungicides recommended for protection of paper and manuscripts, discussed in Chapter IV can be used in herbarium collections also. Heavily infested material may be aired and exposed to sun followed by fumigation with Thymol. Surface application and spraying with suitable fungicides like Pentachlorophenol will prevent fungus attack. Use of thymolized paper for interleaving the herbarium sheets, as recommended for manuscripts, is also a good preventive measure.

Insect Attack

Dried plant material provides a satisfactory nutritional medium for many cellulose feeding insects. According to Fosberg and Sachet (1965) the major pests of herbaria in Europe are Cigarette beetle, *Lasioderma serriocorne* (Fabr), Carpet beetle, *Anthrenus scrophulariae* (C), moths such as *Sterrha bonifata* (Hulst), *Sterrha inquinata* (Scop) Ephistia cautella (Walker) and Angasta Kuhniella (Zeller), the Book-lice, Liposcelis corrodens Heymons and L. divinatorius (Muller) and the Silver fish, Lepisma saccharina L. Hinton (1945) mentions the Museum beetle, Anthrenus museorum as a major pest of herbaria in temperate regions.

Observations on insect damage to herbarium collections in India show that the major pests are Silver fish, Book lice and some of the wood boring beetle such as the Powder-post beetle. Of these the Silver fish is attracted to the glue and paper rather than plant specimens and the Book lice to the anther of flowers and fungi that may grow on the plant material.

Collections depicting economic botany consist of a large number of plant products such as cereals, nuts, barks and leaves, timber specimens etc. attracting several insect pests if poorly preserved. Notable are the cereal pests such as the Khapra beetle, Trogoderma granarium Everts and the Flour beetles, Tribolium castaneum and Tribolium confusum. Presence of the Carpet beetle, Attagenus gloriosae was also noticed occasionally in some insect infested collections in India. It is not sure whether they inflict damage directly to herbarium specimens or are present to feed on other dead insects and their pupal exuviae.

Other insect pests injurious to botanical specimens reported from the USA include the Sawtoothed Grain Beetle, Oryzaephilus surinamensis (Linnaeus), the Carpet Beetle, Trogoderma inclusum Le Conte and the Spider Beetles belonging to the Coleopteran family Ptinidae (Edwards, Bell and King, 1981).

The most effective method of eliminating insect damage on herbaria is to fumigate the collections periodically with suitable insecticides such as Carbon di-sulphide, methyl bromide, carbon tetrachloride or hydrogen cyanide. Repellent chemicals such as Paradichlorobenzene, Naphthalene or formulations like Paradichlorobenzene – benzene – creosote placed in storage cabinets will keep most insects away. A practice followed in temperate regions to kill insect pests is to expose herbaria for a few hours to a temperature of about 44°C. This is not likely to be useful in tropical countries where the highest temperature in summer normally goes even beyond 45°C.

ZOOLOGICAL SPECIMENS

Deterioration by insect pests in one of the most common and difficult problems in the preservation of zoological specimens. Mould growth is also encountered on dry preserved specimens but is of a lesser magnitude and can be combated by using suitable fungicides and repellents. As mentioned earlier wet preserved zoological specimens are not subjected to biodeterioration if they are preserved properly. The method of wet preservation is used generally in the case of invertebrate animals and some of the vertebrates like fishes, amphibians and reptiles. Feathered and haired animals (birds and mammals) are not normally preserved in liquids unless they are required for anatomical investigations.

One of the precautions needed to be considered in wet preservation, particularly of vertebrate animals in formalin or alcohol is to make sure that some preservative fluid is injected in the stomach of the specimen before it is immersed in the liquied preservative. This is necessary because the stomach contains many bacteria which would become active in a dead animal in the process of putrefaction and as a result of their activity certain gases are evolved inflating the stomach and making the specimen float on the liquid in which it is immersed. Constant replenishing of the liquid in the specimen jars is also required to prevent portions of the specimen being exposed to air and thus causing deterioration to the exposed portion. In cases where the strength of the preservative is inadequate there is the possibility of microbial activity and mould growth on the surface of the liquid resulting in the formation a thin scum. The only method for preventing this when happens is to discard the liquid and use a fresh solution of the preservative.

Insect Pests of Dry-preserved Zoological Material

Dry preserved zoological specimens of all kinds – dehydrated specimens of many invertebrates including insect collections, taxidermy specimens, freeze dried specimens, skins, feathers and felts – however well preserved they may be, are all likely to be attacked by insects of various kinds. Wagstafle and Fiddler (1968) lists the following insects as pests of zoological collections.

(i) Golden Spider Beetle, *Niptus hololeucas*
(ii) Australian Spider Beetle, *Ptinus tectus* Boiel
(iii) Museum Beetle, *Anthrenus museorum* (L) and A. *verbasci* (L)
(iv) Drug-store Beetle, *Stegobium paniceum* (L)
(v) Bacon Beetle, *Dermestes lardarius*
(vi) Brown House-moth, *Borkhausenia pseudospretella*
(vii) Tapestry Moth, *Trichophaga tapetzella* (L)
(viii) Common Clothes Moth, *Tineola bisselliella* (Hum)

The above listing of insect pests is obviously based on the observations of the above referred authors in the United Kingdom and perhaps some other European countries.

According to Kingsolver (1981) the following insects are known to attack dry preserved zoological specimens of one form or the other in the USA.

(i) Cigarette Beetle, *Lasioderma serricorne*
(ii) Drug-store Beetle, *Stegobium peniceum*

(iii) Redlegged Ham Beetle, *Nercobia rufipes*

(iv) Furniture Carpet Beetle, *Anthrenus flavipes*

(v) Varied Carpet Beetle, *Anthrenus verbasci*

(vi) Black Carpet Beetle, *Attagenus megatoma*

(vii) Larder Beetle, *Dermestes lardarius*

(viii) Carpet Beetle, *Reesa vespula*

(ix) Odd Beetle, *Thylodrias contractus*

(x) Cabinet Beetle, *Trogoderma inclusum*

(xi) Spider Beetle, *Ptinidae*

(xii) Confused Flour Beetle, *Tribolium confusum*

(xiii) Case-bearing Clothes Moth, *Tinea pellionella*

(xiv) Webbing Clothes Moth, *Tinea bisselliella*

The major insect pests attacking dry preserved zoological specimens in India are observed to be as follows:

Of the above the most common and formidable pest of animal material in museums in India is the Furniture Carpet Beetle, the larvae of which cause irreparable damage to taxidermy specimens. A large number of pests other than those listed above are bound to be present in tropical humid regions. This is an important area that requires extensive study and research in tropical countries.

Tanners and Taxidermists have been aware of the problem from the very beginning. Preventive measure to avoid insect attack have, therefore, become part of most of the preparatory techniques for dry mounting of zoological specimens. Taxidermy is an example where several insecticidal chemicals have been traditionally in use.

Control Measures

Arsenic compounds have been in use for the protection and preservation of zoological material for a long time. John Rowley (1935) describes the use of a patent poison known as 'Veneno' manufactured in New York and extensively used in hide warehouses to protect dry hides and skins from dermestid beetles and other insect pests. It was made by boiling a mixture of white arsenic (Arsenic trioxide) and sodium carbonate. The resultant solution containing sodium arsenite is a powerful insecticide.

Taxidermists use a large number of chemicals and chemical formulations for the treatment of the skin of fishes, reptiles, birds and mammals during the preparatory process. These vary from the dusting of the inner side of the skin of birds with white arsenic or a mixture of white arsenic and borax to elaborate tanning processes for mammalian skins. Some of these formulations are mentioned below:

Arsenic-borax Powder

A mixture of equal portions by volume of dry white arsenic and powdered borax (Sodium tetraborate) used to apply on the inner side of skins, mostly in bird specimens during the process of taxidermy. It keeps the skin supple and prevents insect attack.

Arsenic-Alum Powder

A mixture of equal portions by volume of white arsenic and powdered alum (potassium aluminium sulphate) used for the same purpose as of the above mixture.

Wagstaffe-Barrow Mixture

A mixture for dry application for bird and mammal skins from the inside made in the following proportion (Wagstaffe and Fiddler, 1968).

Borax powder	- 500 gms
Tannic Acid	- 30 gms
Camphor	- 16 gms
DDT	- 3.5 gms
Beechwood Creosote	- 9 drops

Hornaday's Arsenical Soap

A formulation, recommended as the finest mixture for treatment of bird and mammal skins (Wagstaffe and Fiddler, 1968) made with the following ingredients:

White bar soap (soft vriety)	- 1 kg
Powdered white arsenic	- 1 kg
Subcarbonate of potash	- 190 gms
Camphor	- 150 gms
Alcohol	- 250 cc

Salt-acid Tan Solution

Common salt	- 250 gms
Sulphuric acit	- 30 cc
Water	- 5 litres

(The salt and water to be mixed first and sulphuric acid added to it.)

Sulphonated Neats Foot Oil (Moyer, 1953)

Sulphonated Neat's foot oil	- 1 part
Water	- 1 part

(Water to be warmed a little and mixed with the sulphonated oil).

Alum Solutions (Moyer, 1953)

Water	- 1 gallon
Salt	- ½ lb
Alum	- ¼ lb
Carbolic Acid	- ½ ounce

Rowley's Mixture (for preservation of Antlers in "velvet", Wagstaffe and Fiddler, 1968).

Water	- 1 litre
Glycerin	- 2 litres
Salt	- 400 gms
Alum	- 400 gms
White Arsenic	- 400 gms
Formalin	- 500 ml

Arsenical Paste

White Arsenic	
Zinc oxide	equal quality
Soft soap	

Boil together in water to form a paste. A few crystals of Camphor to be mixed when cool.

The insecticidal chemicals or chemical formulations mentioned above are used for application on the flesh side of the skin in birds and small mammals during the process of taxidermy. In the case of larger animals, however, the skin is tanned to strengthen it as well as to prevent biological deterioration.

Animal specimens preserved by the process of freeze drying are also prove to insect attack. Susceptibility to biodeterioration is more acute in specimens because no chemical treatments are given to the skin as in the case of taxidermy. Furthermore, the body tissues including fats are dried *in situ* and therefore a larger amount of nutritional matter is available for insects to thrive upon. Adequate precautionary measures to prevent insect attack are very essential for freeze-dried zoological specimens.

Use of insecticidal Dusts and Spreays

DDT, BHC and Pyrethrum used in the form of dusts and sprays in storage cabinets can be a precautionary measure to keep insects away. This, however, is not a guarantee against localized insect attack that can take place in specimens. As mentioned earlier insecticidal treatments given while preparing specimens as in taxidermy is a very important preventive measure. But action of dermestids on feather, hair etc. is not ruled out by this treatment. Spraying of insecticides on the surface of specimens is not advisable because of the residues that may be left behind. This then has to be taken care of by other methods such as using repellents and fumigation.

Use of Repellents

Paradichlorobenzene and Naphthalene are the two most commonly used repellent chemicals in zoological collections. The latter is less effective compared to the former.

Wagstaffe and Fiddler (1968) are of the opinion that Paradichlorobenzene has some deleterious effect on certain colours of bird and mammal skins, although there is no conclusive evidence to this effect. Most museums use this chemical in storage boxes and display cases containing dried animal specimens with success.

The British Museum (Natural History), London recommends the use of a mixture of Chloroform, Creosote and Naphthalene (CCN) named as British Museum Mixture as a suitable insect repellent. Observations made in India show that a mixture of Paradichlorobenzene, Benzene and Creosote (PBC) is a highly effective repellent. Edolan U is another mothoproofing agent recommended for application on specimens for repellent action.

Fumigation with suitable chemicals is the best method for eliminating insect pests from affected specimens. A large number of fumigants are available today. Wagstaffe and Fiddler (1968) recommend liquid fumigants such as Ethylene dichloride, Methyl formate or Carbon disulphide. All of them are highly inflammable. A mixture of Ethylene dichloride and carbon tetrachloride (3:1 by volume) is a satisfactory non inflammable mixture. Methyl Bromide is also a very useful fumigant. Periodic inspection of specimens for possible biodeterioration and immediate isolation and treatment of affected materials is necessary to ensure proper preservation of biological materials in museums.

Chapter VI

USE OF INSECTICIDES AND FUNGICIDES

The treatment of museum objects against biodterioration follows two general courses of actions: (1) 'Preventive mesaures' aimed at forestalling the possibilities of infestation and (2) 'Control measures' required to be undertaken once infestation has already taken place. The use of fungicies and insecticides for the above purposes with reference to different kinds of museum objects has been discussed in Chapters IV and V. Some general considerations, criteria for use and evaluation of biocides are discussed in this chapter.

Preventive Measures

The necessity for museums to adopt proper preventive measures to avoid biodeterioration has been emphasized throughout. These primarily consist of "good house-keeping practices" that prevent opportunities for fungi, insects, rodents etc. to survive inside the premises. Prevention should also be aimed against the danger of infestation from outside the museum.

Most organic museum materials require some kind of chemical treatment or protection against biological agents of deterioration. Tapestries, paintings, antiquities, extensive collections of insects, mounted specimens all are likely prey for insects unless precautionary measures are taken. Many museums are housed in older types of "run-down" buildings which are ideally suited for invasion by termites and other wood eaters.

Factors that are to be considered in respect of prevention of biodeterioration can conveniently be discussed under two heads: 1) Chemical treatments given to the objects themselves and 2) the use of chemicals within display and storage unit to repel biological agencies. To the first category belongs the use of chemicals incorporated in the preparation of specimens and/or chemical treatments given before an object is displayed or stored. Examples are the use of arsenic compounds in the preparation of taxidermy specimens discussed in Chapter V and the sterilization of wood, textiles etc. mentioned in Chapter IV. The second category deals with the use of chemicals within museum show-cases or storage vaults to repel biological agents. An example is the use of appropriate repellents such as Paradichlorobenzene.

Use of Repellents: In spite of the preventive treatments given to an object during preparation or before installation in a museum, there is an added need for creating an atmosphere around the object which will repel insects, fungi etc. Some of the chemicals commonly used for this purpose and Naphthalene, Paradichlorobenzene, Thymol, Saffrol, Camphor etc. Certain special formulations are also used. The volatile chemicals like Naphthalene and Paradichlorobenzene vapourize slowly, and the vapours are sustained in a show-case, if it is airtight. But, they would be effective only if the required amount of vapour concentration in the show case is maintained. It is also necessary to remember that while using a chemical like Paradichlorobenzene, the fumes of which are relatively heavy, it shuld be placed at the top of the show case, not only at the bottom. These are important aspects to consider. Though Naphthalene and Paradichlorobenzene may not kill insects readily, they can do so if used in greater concentrations as in the case of fumigation. As a repellent, Naphthalene seems less effective, probably due to the increased resistance being developed by insects. It generally reported that Paradichlorobenzene is more effective that Naphthalene.

A simple experiment was conducted to find out the comparative efficiency of these two chemicals to kill insects when used in sufficient concentrations. The Petri-dishes of 150 cc. capacity each were used. Five gms. of Paradichlorobenzene was placed in one and 5 gms. of Naphthalene placed in the other. Then 20 mature larvae of the Dermestid beetle, Trogoderma granarium Everts were introduced in each of them. The containers were made airtight by using scotch tape. It was observed that whereas it took 18 hours for all the larvae in the dish containing Paradichlorobenzene to die, those in Naphthalene died after only 2 ½ days. This shows that the former is much more effective in terms of biocidal qualities.

A formulation known as British Museum Mixture or C.C.N. is recommended by the British Museum (Natural History) as a repellent for insect collections. The mixture is made by first preparing a saturated solution of Nabhthalene in chloroform and then mixing with an equal quantity of Creosote. This repellent has been found to be useful also for the protection of several organic materials, particularly ethnographic objects like reeds, basketry etc.

The presence of Chloroform in the above mixture makes it unsuitable for use with materials like dyed textiles, certain beautifully coloured Lepidopteran specimens etc. because a slight fading effect on colours has been noticed. With a view to formulating a repellent mixture which could be generally used in museum storage, several combinations of chemicals were tried. Based on odservations made, the following formulation is recommended as an effective repellent. The mixture is named P.B.C. and is made with the following ingredients:

Paradechlorobebzene	50gms.
Benzene	50c.c
Creosote	50c.c

This is found very effective against Dermestid beetles, Cockroaches, book-worms, wood eating insects like Termites, Wood borers etc. In sufficient quantities it also has proved to be a good fumigant.

Control Measures

Once infestation has already taken place, control measures must be resorted to. The use of insecticides and fungicides is a rapidly developing and changing field. Particularly in the last few years this field has undergone a profound transformation as a result of progress in the production of a great number of synthetic compounds with lasting toxic action against the biological agents of deterioration. The ability of some insect pests to develop resistance against insecticidal chemicals is another factor that poses a challenge. Many insects are capable of successfully adapting themselves for coexistence with pesticides. Therefore, newer and more efficient insecticides are constantly being introduced. Though a large variety of biocides are available in the market, all are not suitable for use in a museum. Many of the pesticides used in agriculture and commerce in the form of sprays, baits etc. have little utility in this context. But museum Conservators can draw upon the advances in knowledge in these fields and adapt them for use in the museum.

COMMON INSECTICIDES

Based on how they act insecticides are classified into 'Stomach Poisons', 'Contact Poisons' or 'Respiratory Poisons' This classification is based on the mode of entry of the poison and its manner of action as discussed earlier. Another grouping is based on the chemical nature of insecticides as inorganic poison, organic compounds derived from plants, synthetic organic compounds etc. Insects with chewing, sponging, lapping or siphoning mouth parts are often more readily destroyed by poisoning their food than by other means. Contact poisons are generally employed for control of insects with piercing and sucking mouth parts. The insect should come in direct contact with these insecticides to be killed. This may occur by direct application to the body or by the residual effect of the poison upon the surface where the insect crawls or rests. Respiratory poisons are released as gases in an enclosed chamber, the process known as 'Fumigation'. It is very effective means of killing insects if the correct dosage is administered for an appropriate period of time.

The classification of insecticides is a matter to be considered as one for convenience only because many overlap in qualities as well as in mode of action. Some of the more important chemicals generally used for pesticidal operations in museums are discussed below.

Arsenic Compounds

Arsenic compounds are the most important and most widely used stomach poison for insect control in museums. Arsenic (arsenic tri oxide or Arsenious oxide) is a very active poison and is extensively used by Taxidermists in their preparation work. Arsenic pastes have been used in the past as well as at present in Taxidermy. Arsenic compounds often act as stomach poisons as well as contact poisons. Because of their high toxicity special care must be taken while handling any arsenic preparation.

Fluorine Compounds

Sodium fluoride is a compound usually used as an insecticide, particularly against cockroaches. A hot 4% acqueous solution of Sodium fluoride is often used for insect proofing of wooden objects. This chemical also has fungicidal properties. Zinc silico fluoride is another fluorine compound very much used for the sterilization of stone against vegetative growth.

Pyrethrum

pyrethrum is a contact insecticide with rapid "knock-down" action It is derived from the flowers of the Chrysanthemum plant, Pyrethrum cinerariaefolium. Formulations of Pyrethrum in dusts, aerosols and solutions as well as emulsions are commercially available, particularly in the U.S.A. Pyrethrum is one of those rare insecticides that is the most toxic to insects and least toxic to human beings. Plenderleith(1956) recommends a mixture of pyrethrum and D.D.T. in a spray solution for the protection of leather objects from insect attack . This chemical in a Benzene base, or a mixture of it and D.D.T in Benzene, was found by the author to be a good insecticide against dermestid beetles. It is also recommended for the treatment of several different kind of museum materials (see Chapter V).

D.D.T. (Dichloro-diphenyl-trichloroethane)

D.D.T. is a chlorinated synthetic organic insecticide. In its pure form it is a white powder. It is less toxic than Sodium fluoride and act as a contact poison. D.D.T. does not repel insects, but acts upon the nervous system. Although some insects may survive several hours in D.D.T., this chemical is most effectives in spray solutions. Benzeme or Keosine are the best for the purpose. D.D.T. is also used successfully in mixtures with other chemicals like Pyrethrum.

B.H.C. (Benzene Hexachloride)

This chlorinated organic insecticide is commercially know as Gammaxene in India, and Lindane in the U.S.A. In insecticidal properties, B.H.C. is almost similar to D.D.T. but more toxic to certain insects. In this case also spray solutions are more effective.

Carbon-disulphide

Carbon-disulphide is one of the best fumigants for museum objects when adequate precaution against fire is taken. It is a colourless liquid with a boiling pointof 46.3 degrees centigrade. The pure chemical has a sweetish, not unpleasant odour, but the commercial grade is often yellowish in colour due to the excess of Sulphur and has a disagreeable odour due to the Hydrogen Sulphide it contains. Carbon disulphide is very poisonous to human beings, producing giddiness, vomiting, congestion, coma and even death if breathed in concentrated form for a long period. Another undesirable property of Carbon di-sulphide is that it is highly inflammable. Sometimes Carbon tetrachloride is mixed with it to reduce the fire hazard.

Carbon Tetrachloride

This is also a colourless liquid, but noninflammable and possessing a pungent aromatic odour. Its boiling point is 76.8 degrees centigrade. It evaporates slowly and has a considerable insecticidal action. It has an anaesthetic effect upon man, and while not highly toxic in weak concentrations, care should be taken no to expose oneself to the fumes for extended periods.

Methyl Bromide

Methyl Bromide is a comparatively recent addition to the list of insect fumigants and it has already obtained a place of importance in Western countries, particularly in the U.S.A. It is a liquid that boils at 4 to 4.5 degrees centigrade, a factor that makes it difficult to store and use in the tropical countries. In toxicity Methyl Bromide compares favourably with Hydrocyanic acid, Chloropicrin or Ethylene dioxide. It is, therefore, a very useful fumigant which is all the more effective when used in the presence of moisture. Unfortunately, from the toxicological point of view it is also dangerous to man. Because of its high toxicity, high volatility and lack of warning properties such as odour or irritation it is quite hazardous to handle. Handling and use therefore must be carried out in such a way that exposure does not occur or is limited to intensity levels known to be safe.

Because of the difficulty in storing as well as using this quickly volatile chemical under tropical conditions, another very closely related chemical, Ethyl Bromide was tried in our labouratory for insect control. It has almost the same toxicological properties. The boiling point is 80 degrees centigrade and therefore, is easy to store and use under tropical conditions.

Hydrocyanic Acid

This is a colourless volatile liquid boiling at 26 degrees centigrade. It is inflammable and burns like alcohol when ignited. The toxic action of the compound to living organisms is due to the inhibiting effect it has upon oxidation of the cells. It arrests the activity of all forms of living matter. Hydrocyanic acid enters into a chemical combination with the iron content of Cytochrome, a respiratory catalyst in blood and renders it incapable of performing its function. This chemical, therefore, is a very effective insecticidal fumigant. Because of its high toxicity it can be handled only by very competent operators and where special fumigation chambers are available for the purpose. Hydrocyanic acid is used for the fumigation of museum objects only where such facilities are available.

Sulphur Di-oxide

Sulphur di-oxide is perhaps the oldest fumigant known to man and was used in flour mills for insect disinfestations. But the danger of fire, corrosive action of the chemical on metals etc. have prevented it from becoming a popular fumigant. It marketed in liquid form in Cylinders. It is also highly toxic in nature.

Trichloroethylene

This is a heavy, colourless, non-inflammable liquid boiling at 88 degrees Centigrade. It is quite similar in toxicity to Carbon tetra Chloride and is used either alone or in combination with other chemicals as a fumigant. Like other chlorinated hydrocarbons, this one is also harmful if breathed in.

Naphthalene

This is the chemical repellent most widely used in museums in India. Its effectiveness is often negligible, particularly when the required vapour concentration is not taken into account. Naphthalene is a white crystalline substance that sublimes slowly on exposure to air.

Paradichlorobenzene

This also is a white crystalline material that sublimes slowly on exposure to air. It vapourizes much quicker than Naphthalene. The vapours are not considered to be harmful to man, though it is not advisable to expose oneself to a concentration of the gas. As an insect repellent it is one of the best chemicals to use in a museum. The vapours are heavier than air and therefore, it should be placed in such a way that the show-case will have a continuous supply of vapour from above.

TOXICOLOGICAL EVALUATION OF SOME INSECTICIDES

With a view to understanding the comparative efficiency and toxicological properties of some of thee commonly used stomach poisons, contact poisons, fumigants and repellents an experiment was conducted by exposing some insect larvae in several chemicals and chemical formulations. Containers of uniform size (Petri dishes – 100 cc) were used and white blotting papers were placed on each of them over which 20 larvae (mature) each of the Khapra Beetle, Trogoderma granarium were released. One cc., or one gm., of the various chemicals were administered, each container having different insecticides. The duration taken for mortality of the larvae in all cases was observed and noted. The containers were kept airtight with the help of scotch tape during the periods of observation. The Khapra larva was selected for this study because it is a dermestid species and demestid beetles are among the most harmful of insect pests in India. The results obtained will also be applicable to other species of this group. Further, the Khapra larva is known to be very resistant to several insecticides. The results of the study are represented in the following table:

TOXICOLOGICAL EVALUATION OF SOME INSECTICIDES

Larval species: *Trogoderma granarium* Everts No. Introduced: 20 ech

Insecticide used	*Mortality rate (No. of deaths)*			*Remarks*
	1st hr.	*2nd hr.*	*3rd hr.*	
Paradichlorobenzene	-	-	-	Died only after 18 hours
Naphthalene	-	-	-	Died only after 60 hours.
Benzene hexa Chloride	3	8	12	Complete mortality after 6 hours.
D.D.T	2	5	7	Complete mortality after within 1/2 hour.

Insecticide used	*Mortality rate (No. of deaths)*			*Remarks*
	1st hr.	*2nd hr.*	*3rd hr.*	
B.H.C. in Benzene (10%)	18	20	-	Death starts within 1/2 hour.
C.C.N.	16	20	-	Death starts within 1/2 hours
P.B.C.	18	20	-	Death starts within 15 minutes
Carbon di-Sulphide	20	-	-	Death starts within 5 minutes
Carbon tetra Chloride	20	-	-	Death starts within 5 minutes
Ethyl Bromide	20	-	-	Death starts within 5 minutes
Trichloroethylene	20	-	-	Death starts within 5 minutes
Ethyiene di-Chloride	20	-	-	Death starts within 5 minutes.

The above observations show that fumigants like Carbon di- Sulphide, Carbon tetra Chloride, Ethyl Bromide, Trichloroethylene, Ethylene di-Chloride etc. are more effective than contact insecticides. Repellents like Paradichlorobenzene and Naphthalene do not have rapid killing action. Of the two, Paradichlorobenzene is far more effective. It was also observed that contact insecticides like D.D.T. and B.H.C. are more effective when used in spray solutions. Formulations like C.CN. and P.B.C. are to be preferred as repellents over paradichlorobenzene or Naphthalene alone. Of the two, P.B.C., a formulation devised and recommended by the author Ethyl Bromide can be used as an insect fumigant advantageously in tropical countries like India. It is Particularly effective in the extermination of dermestid beetles.

How Insecticides Act

Insecticides to be able to kill insects must enter the body and reach vital organs. Poisons like the arsenical compounds when eaten by insects enter the digestive tracts. Such stomach poisons can be effective only if eaten and therefore are useful to control insects with chewing mouth parts such as beetles, crickets etc. Fumigants are gaseous poisons which enter the insect body through the respiratory system or the body wall. They can kill all types of insects. Contact insecticides enter through penetrating the body wall or the breathing tubes and have a quick action.

Modern insecticides like D.D.T., B.H.C. etc., enter the body in more than one way, often in all the above three ways. The insect body has a protective outer layer called the 'exoskeleton' which is stiff and hard on the dorsal side. The body wall of this exoskeleton is composed of a layer of waxy material, called the epicuticle. Under this waxy layer there is a thick layer composed of chitin and protein, the exocuticle. Underneath this there is the flexible endocuticle. Beneath this is the cellular layer and the basement membrane (Fig.). The body wall plays a very important part in respect of the insect's reaction to the insecticide. The body hairs present in many insects keep insecticide dusts from coming in contact with the body wall. The epicuticle is the most important barrier for most insecticides. It is capable of repelling water borne insecticides because of its waxy layer. But, oil borne or organic solvent borne insecticides are very effective because they dissolve the epicuticle. The effectiveness of the insecticides is correlated with the thickness of the body wall components and the nearness of vital parts (Howell, 1960) Antennae, where some of the sense organs are situated, mouth parts, inter-segmental membranes and legs are also vulnerable areas.

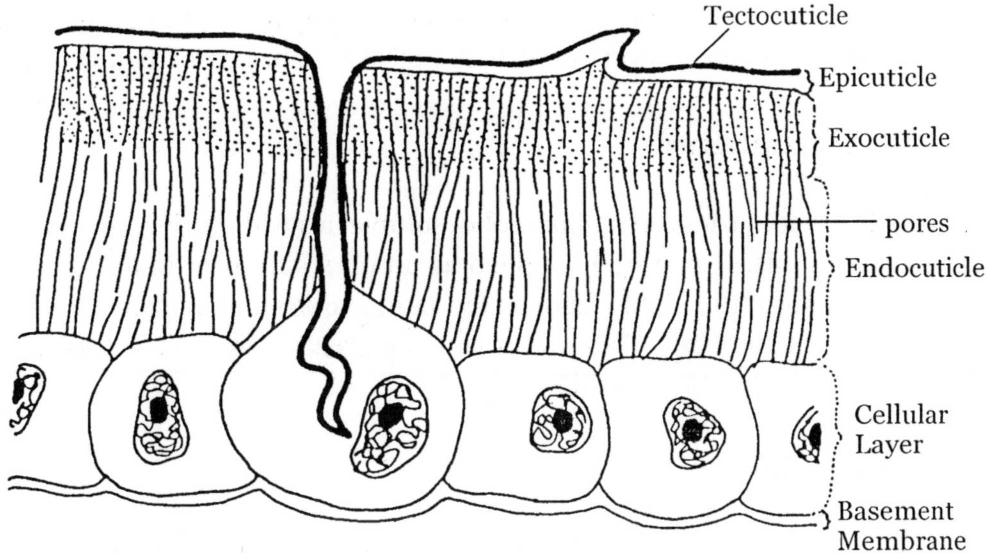

Diagrammatic cross section of Insect body wall.

Insecticides such as DDT, Pyrethrum etc., when dissolved in fats and oils, penetrate and kill insects more rapidly than water soluble chemicals. Lime and other caustic materials also cause speedy kill of insects. Gaseous insecticides enter the insect body through respiratory openings called spiracles leading into the breathing tubes or trachea. They attack the respiratory system and render the insect unable to use the oxygen brought into its body.

COMMON FUNGICIDES

No single fungicide possesses al the desired characteristics for use in museums. Fungus spores are often very resistant to toxic substances and most chemicals which would kill them are undesirable for use in the museum because they are corrosive, give off objectionable odours or are highly poisonous to human beings. Some of the most commonly used fungicides for the protection of museum objects are discussed below:

Pentachlorophenol

This is a colourless crystalline solid, soluble in a wide variety of organic solvents and oils. It is usually applied as an oil solution or in an organic solvent. Because it is highly chlorinated pentachlorophenol is better used in presence of an alkali. This would act as a precaution against probable liberation of Hydrochloric acid.

Paranitrophenol

This is also a very effective fungicide for use on museum materials where its yellowish colour may not be considered objectionable. This chemical is very much favoured for the protection of leather objects. Usually it is used as a spray solution prepared (very low concentration) in paraffin distillate.

Salicylanilide

This is commercially sold under the name 'Shirlan' and is very much used for the protection of paper and textiles from fungus attack. A white crystalline chemical, it can be used in aquous or non-aquous solutions.

Mercuric Chloride

Mercuric Chloride (Corrosive sublimate) is widely used as a fungicide in herbarium preparations in museums. Because of its corrosive nature it is not usually favoured for the treatment of other kinds of museum objects, though occasionally it is used for the treatment of paper affected by fungus growth. Used either in aquous or alcoholic solutions.

Zinc Chloride

This is a white, deliquescent substance, very much soluble in water. It is also soluble in alcohol. A concentrated solution of Zinc Chloride is used for impregnating wood to prevent biodeterioration. It is also used on monuments and stone sculptures affected by cryptogamic plant growth.

Thymol

This is the most widely accepted chemical for the fumigation of archival material affected by fungus growth. It can be used also as a fungus repellent, as a spray when dissolved in alcohol or as thymolated paper. Thymol vapours are pungent and contact with the chemical causes irritation on the skin.

Apart from the above, Zinc silico fluoride and Saffrol are also used for the prevention of fungus growth on museum objects. There are many other fungicidal chemicals too, but only a brief outline of the use of fungicides is intended here.

Evaluation of Fungicides

Fungi vary enormously in their response to toxic chemicals. Some fungi can tolerate surprisingly high concentrations of certain fungicides while other fungi will be eliminated with quite low concentrations of the same fungicide. Low percentage of thymol and safrol were found to inhibit the growth of *Aspergillus niger* whereas they had little effect on certain *Penicillium* species. Paranitrophenol and zinc sillco fluoride were found effective against *Pencillium* but not against *Aspergillus*. Such variations in tolerance to poisons imply that it is essential to use as many test fungi as possible in carrying out laboratory tests of toxicity. It is obvious that effective use of fungicides calls for an understanding of the identity of species so that appropriate fungicides will be selected. The optimum percentages of the fungicides required may also vary depending on the fungi and the toxicity of the chemical.

With a view to finding out which of the fungicides would be effective against most species of fungi, and what should be the optimum requirements for the desired effect, the present experimental study was undertaken.

The following chemicals were tested for effectiveness:

1. Mercuric chloride
2. Sodium salicylate
3. Pentachlorophenol
4. Paranitrophenol
5. Sodium pentachlorophenate
6. Safrol
7. Thymol
8. Zinc chloride
9. Zinc silicofluoride
10. Formalin
11. Sodium fluoride
12. Ammonia
13. Carbolic acid

When using fungicides on museum objects one has to consider the possible chemical effects of the toxic material on the object; any damaging effect has to be avoided. From this point of view, it is always necessary to use the lowest concentration of the chemical that would still be fungicidal. The first set of experiments were designed to see which of the above fungicides would be effective in one percent solutions. The optimum lower limits and upper limits required for each of the chemicals, in terms of fungicidal properties, wee worked out through further experiments.

Preparation of Test Materials

Watman's filter paper cut into small strips (1″× 3″) were used as text materials. These samples were treated by immersing them for 30 minutes in each of the fungicidal solutions. They were then dried in air and in oculated with fungus spores for testing. Some untreated controls were used for comparison.

Preparation of the Innoculum

Fungus spores from a heavily infected paper manuscript containing more than 75% of the species mentioned earlier were removed by washing them into boiled and cooled tap water. The spores were allowed to settle down, and then decanted. One drop each of the water containing spores was put in the middle of the test sample strips with a pipette. The innoculum was allowed to dry on the strip for one hour before subjecting it to the test.

Test Method

The 'Seeded Agar Plate method' recommended by Sykes (1959) was used as the test method. The culture medium, PDA, was prepared and a thin layer of the medium was poured on sterilized Petri-dishes and allowed to gel. Each of the inoculated paper strips was now placed on the medium in the Petri-dishes and another layer of the medium to cover the strip was poured. The Petri-dishes were closed with their covers and were left to develop fungus growths. Growth, if any, in each case was observed daily form the second day onwards and results were analysed on the seventh day.

DISCUSSION OF THE RESULTS

Fungicidal Properties of One Percent Solutions of the Chemicals Tested

Based on growth observed, if any, in each of the samples treated with 1%solutions of the chemicals, their respective effectiveness were recorded. The foolowing table shows the results of observations made:

Chemical 1%	*Solvent used*	*Nature of growth* *- No growth* *+ Scanty growth* *++ Profiuse growth* *+++ Very profuse growth*
Mercuric chloride	Water	-
Sodium salicylate	Water	++
Pentachlorophenol	Alcohol	-
Paranitrophenl	Alcohol	+
Sodium pentachlorophenate	Water	++
Safrol	Alcohol	+++
Thymol	Alcohol	++
Zinc chloride	Water	+++
Zinc silicofluoride	Water	+++
Formalin	Water	++
Sodium fluroride	Water	++
Ammonia	Water	+++
Carbolic acid	Water	+++

From the above it can be observed that only mercuric chloride and pentachlorophenol are effective at one percent solution wheras the others all showed varying degrees of fungus growth.

Further experiments were therefore conducted to establish optimum limits of percentages (either lower or higher) of the other chemicals. In those cases where effectiveness was not obtained even at 25% solution, no further experiments were done as such percentages could not be used on museum objects. The following table gives the optimum effective percentages of all the chemicals.

Chemical	*Solvent*	*Optimum effective %*
Mercuric chloride	Water	0.2
Pentachlorophenol	Alcohol	0.25
Paranitrophenol	Alcohol	3.0
Sodium fluroride	Water	5.0
Thymol	Alcohol	5.0
Sodium salicylate	Water	10.0
Sodium Pentachlorophenate	Water	10.0
Safrol	Alcohol	Above 25%
Zinc chloride	Water	"
Zinc silicofluoride	Water	"
Formalin	Water	"
Ammonia	Water	"
Carbolic acid	Water	"

Results of the Study

The results of the study can be summarized as follows:

(i) Mercuric chloride and pentachlorophenol are effective at very low concentrations of 0.2 and 0.25 percentages respectively.

(ii) Paranitrophenol is effective only at 3% and above.

(iii) Thymol and sodium fluoride are effective at and above the 5% level.

(iv) Sodium salicylate and sodium pentachlorophenate are effective at 10% or above.

(v) Other chemicals tested require much higher percentage which are beyond the limits of safety as far as museum materials are concerned.

The above observations are with reference to the optimum percentages of fungicides required to be effective against all species of fungi. However, mention must be made of some remarkable factors noticed during the course of the experiment. A chemical at a given lower percentage may inhibit the growth of some species of fungi while permitting others to freely grow. This calls for further experimentations to arrive at optimum percentages required to inhibit each specific species.

Another important aspect which needs further investigations is to find out the chemical effect of each of the fungicides on different museum materials so as to be able to recommend the use of individual fungicides for specific materials.

Precautions and Safety Rules for using Biocides

The use of insecticides and fungicides in museums, libraries and archives necessitates a number of special considerations. The first consideration should be that these institutions are frequented and used by people. Introducing poisonous gases, liquids or solids into such premises can be a hazardous business. Unless all dangerous eventualities are adequately safeguarded, the possibility exists that it may be harmful to people. An excellent paper by Piero Gallo (1963) entitled, 'Problems in the use of insecticides in occupied premises' deserves mention in this context.

Safety and safety rules call for prior planning and cannot be left to chance. All those who handle pesticides must be safety conscious at every stage of their control operation. Technical training of those who carry out disinfestations work is of fundamental importance. It is imperative that they be accustomed to such work, know the risks involved, know the effective methods for preventing poisoning and basic first aid measures.

Safety Check List

The following list includes some of the important considerations when dealing with chemical disinfestants in museums and related institutions.

(i) Store all pesticides in original containers and in a locked cupboard.

(ii) Read the label and pay attention to precautions.

(iii) Keep all pesticides away from food or foodstuffs.

(iv) Employ chemical disinfestants only when needed, using the correct one only at the optimum lethal dose required.

(v) Do not inhale pesticide dusts or sprays.

(vi) Avoid spilling pesticides on skin or clothing. If spilled, wash off at once with soap and water. Particles or drops of chemicals got into the eyes should be flushed out immediately with a large volumes of clean water.

(vii) Do not eat or smoke when working with pesticides.

(viii) Discard all pesticide containers without labels or with damaged or illegible labels. Do not guess at contents.

(ix) Use protection equipment such as gas masks and respirators when necessary.

(x) Make sure that adequate fresh air and ventilation is available in places where pesticide operations are carried out.

(xi) Know first aids for poisoning.

In spite of all precautions accidental poisoning can occur, in which case one should know what should be done immediately. Regardless of how the poisoning occurred, prompt and efficient remedial action is called. The first action should be to call a doctor at once. If one is unable to reach a physician, or until he or she arrives there are a few first-aid measures that can be applied. Donald Fvear (1967) summarises these first aid measures as follows:

(i) If the poison has been swallowed, empty the stomach immediately. As a first aid measure vomiting may be induced by putting a finger or a tongue depressor down the patient's throat. An emetic such as warm salt solution, ground mustard (1 teaspoonful in a glass of warm water) or syrup of ipecac (same amount in water). However, never try to make on an conscious person vomit. After the stomach has been emptied, give a demulcent, such as raw eggs, milk, or a thin flour paste. These serve to absorb the poison and to soothe irritated membranes. Do not give oil.

(ii) If the poison has been spilled on the skin or clothing, remove clothing and scrub skin thoroughly with soap and warm water.

(iii) If the poison has been inhaled as in the case of a toxic fumigant, remove patient to the open air and give artificial respiration (preferable mouth to mouth) if the patient is not breathing.

Chapter VII

SOME GENERAL CONSIDERATIONS

The existence of every living organism is dependant upon the availability of food and optimum environmental conditions. The growth and population of an organism increases when these conditions become favourable. Organisms like bacteria, fungi and insects that cause deterioration to museum materials are no exceptions.

As a dominant species in his environment, man endeavours to keep others under control, particularly, those that are injurious to his person and property. In trying to prevent and control the deleterious activities of living organism on museum materials, man is attempting to protect the evidence of his cultural and natural heritage including his artistic, scientific and technological achievements. It was with a view to throwing some light on the problems of biodeterioration of such materials that the present treatise was undertaken. The correct identification of the species and a knowledge of the life history and habitats of the biological agency of deterioration is the essential pre-requiste for any systematic attempt on control measures.

Apart from the chemical control measures discussed earlier, there is a need for controlling the environment so as not to provide conditions favourable for the growth of the agencies of biodeterioration. Temperature and humidity control in a museum, therefore, is a matter of great practical importance. Observations made in various countries of the world have shown that temperature restricted to between 16 and 20 degrees centigrade and relative humidity varying between 40 and 60 percent are ideal for the preservation of almost all kinds of museum materials. Under these environmental conditions, bacteria, fungi and insects have little chances of active growth and development and fortunately the above conditions are also suitable for human comforts. There are several methods available for the control of temperature and humidity. The attainment of the above conditions can be brought about most successfully by air-conditioning. But, when technical or economical considerations make it impossible to have air-conditioning, other methods (both physical and chemical) should be resorted to.

There is no two opinion about the fact that 'prevention is better than cure'. Preventive methods, apart from ensuring proper environmental conditions, includes the strategic placement of repellents to keep the organism away. as a matter of fact, the use of repellents should be considered as the best solution to the problem of preventing biodeterioration in the museum. Although, there are no repellents that are hundred percent effective, progress has been made in the development of more effective repellents in recent years. Paradichlorobenzene could be accepted as a useful, safe and dependable repellent. A vapour concentration of atleast 3 m.g. per litre of air is required for best results. It is also to be remembered that the fumes of paradichlorobenzene are heavier than air while deciding where to keep it in a cabinet. C.C.N. is also a very useful repellent, particularly for biological specimens. P.B.C. the formulation recommended by the author has shown promising results as an all-purpose repellent. Thymol is considered as a good fungus repellent and is used either dry or in a solution of alcohol. Even with these precautionary measures one cannot afford to overlook the necessity of periodical checking and observation of the collections to detect biological attack. Any new incoming material, particularly the kind of objects like ethnographical materials, biological collections of birds, mammals, insects etc. should be subjected to suitable fumigation treatments before they are placed in storage or on display.

When infestation has already taken place, control measures as referred to in the previous chapter have to be resorted to. Suitable methods are administered only after a careful study of the composition of the object affected, the kind of living organism responsible for the damage, the nature of alteration suffered by the object, the particular life-cycle stage in which the organism exists, the suitability of the chemical to be employed and its toxicity and chemical reaction in terms of the object, the enemy and the operator. It must be emphasized that the use of chemicals in museum premises should not add to environmental pollution through insecticides. In many cases, satisfactory solutions involve the coordinated application of information from several widely separated disciplines. A problem in preservation of paper, for example, may concern with facts from such fields as organic chemistry, physical chemistry, paper technology, taxonomy, ecology and bionomics of paper destroying organisms, and the toxicology relating to the biocides to be used. Such inter-disciplinary cooperation of biologists, chemists, technologists, toxicologists and the conservation scientists is often necessary for a proper understanding of the problem and for evolving a suitable solution. The conservation specialist working in a Museum is seldom equipped with such an all-round knowledge in these diverse fields. It is neither possible nor can be expected. He, therefore, has to obtain the necessary technical help form other sources.

The role of the biologist deserves special mention in this context. He has the task of identifying the species responsible for the damage. He has to employ a number of laboratory techniques and methods in identifying as well as studying these organisms. He maintains cultures of fungi and insects to study their characteristics. The life cycle of the pests, their feeding habits, their potential threat to various kinds of museum materials etc. are studied by him through experimentation and research. It must be again emphasized that such knowledge of life processes and characteristics of the several agencies of biodeterioration forms the basic foundation on which systematic and intelligent control measures could rest.

Several problems of biodeterioration still await solution. The physico-chemical effects of various fungicides and insecticides on different museum materials remains to be fully investigated. The feeding habits and potential threat of many of the pests need further study. Safe and efficient use of biocides to control different organisms affecting various kinds of materials call for continued efforts. The whole field of chemical conservation vs biological activity, thus, is a promising one for further research.

In concluding this study of biodeterioration of museum materials and control measures it may be stated that we are only at the beginning of exploring a vast field of study.

BIBLIOGRAPHY

Adema, D.M.M. Hazeu, W, Hueck-Vander Plas, Hueck, H.J. Vander Toorn, J. and Waterman, H.A. (1955) Recent Developments in Biodeterioration Research, TNO Central Laboratorium Communication No. 229. Delft, Netherlands.

Alexopoulos, C.J. and Bold, H.C. (1967) Algae & Fungi, Macmillan, New York.

Ambler, H.R. and Finney, C.F. (1957). Brown stain formed on wet cellulose – *Nature*, 179: II4I

Anderson, Roger F. (1960). Forest and Shade Tree Entomology, John Wlley & Sons, New York and London.

Anon. (1964). The Common Furniture Beetle (*Anobium Punctatum* de Geer) Pamphlet 13, New South Wales Forestry Comission, Division of Wood Technology, Sydney.

Ayyeppa, P.K. Cheema, P.S. and Perti, S.L. (1957). A life-history study of *Anthrenus flavipes* Lec. (Col., Dermestidae) – *Bull. Ant. Res.* 49, pp. 185-198.

Back, E.A. (1920) Book Lice or Psocids; Annoying household pests, U.S. Dept. of Agriculture, Bulletin No. 11.4.

Back, E.A. (1938) Carpet Beetles, Leaflet 150, U.S.D.A., Washington D.C.

Back, E.A. (1947) – Book Worms, The Indian Archives, 1:2.

Back, E.A. (1947) Clothes Moths, Leaflet 145, U.S.D.A. Washington D.C.

Ballou, H.A., (1912). Insect pests of the Lesser Antilles. Pamphlet series No. 71, Imperial Department of Agriculture for the West Indies, Bridgetown, Barbados.

Barnes, J.H. and Grove A.J. (1916) – The insects attacking stored wheat in Punjab and methods of compating them, including a chapter on the chemistry of respiration – *Mem. Dep. Agrio.* (Chem. ser.) 4:165.

Barnes, J.M. (1970) Toxic hazards from wood preservatives', International Pest Control XII, 5, 20.

Bayer J. (1908) Insect Enemies of Books, Scientific American, Vol. 98.

Beckwith, T.D. Swanson, W.H. and Iams, T.M. (1940) – Deterioration of Paper: the cause and effect of Foxing, Publi. Univ. Calif. boil. Sci., 1: 13 pp. 299-356.

Belyakova, L.A. and Petrova, L.G. (1964), 'Mould Fungi' on Books and their control, collection of materials on the preservation of Library resources. Translated from Russian and published by the national Science Foundation, Washington D.C.

Block, S.S. (1591) 'Protection of Paper and Textiles from insect damage', Ind. Engng. Chem, 43.

Block, S.S. (1951) 'Experiments in mildew prevention' *Mod. Sanit*, 3, 61-67.

Brazzel, J.R. (1951) 'How to control Silverfish' Clothes moths and Cerpet beetles', *Pest Control*, Vol. 27, No.1.

British Museum (Natural History) (1920), Furniture Beetles – their life history and how to check or prevent damages caused by the warm, economic series No. 11, British Museum (N.H.)

British Museum (Natural History (1950), Clothes Moths and House Moths – their life history, habits and control, 5th Ed., British Museum (N.H., London.

Casey, P.S. (1982) 'The isolation and identification of fungi on Ethnographic artefacts' International Biodeterioration Bulletin, Vol. 18, No. 2.

Cerwinska, E and Sadurska, J. (1953) Actinomycetes damaging old manuscripts and documents, *Acts Microbiol.* pol. Vol. II.

Cheema, P.S. (1956). Studies on the bionomics of the Case-bearing Clothes Moth, *Tipea pellionella* (L), Bull. Ent. Res. 47:167.

Churchill, A.V. (1963) Microbial fuel tank corrosion; mechanisms and contributing factors, Materials Protection, 2, 19-23.

War, C.B. (1963) corrosion resulting from microbial fuel tank contamination, Materials Protection 2, 10-16.

Collins, P.B. (1936) Household pests, their habits, prevention and control, Pitman, London.

Da Costa, E.W.B. and Osborne D. Lynette, (1969)An evaluation of preservatives for the superficial treatment of Wood. J. *Institute Wood Science*, Vol. IV. No. 6.

Daifuku, Hiroshi. (1968) The significance of cultural Property, The conservation of Cultural Property Unesco.

Dayal, H.M. Dixit, V.N. and Agrawal, P.N. (1970) Microbial attack on glass slides and its prevention, *Research and Industry* Vol. 15, No. 4.

Edwards, R. Stephen, Bell, M. Bruce and King Blizabetha Mary (1981) Pest control in Museums. The Association of Systematics Collections, U.S.A.

E. Humann, R. Norman (1961) a new method for control of Powder Post Beetles, *Pest Control*, June 1961).

Ellis, D. (1919), Iron Bacteria, London: Methuen.

Evans, Dorothy M. (1849). The protection of books against Insects, Eng. Bull. 9.

Evans, D.M. (1966) 'The deterioration of Book-binding materials in the Tropics', Society of chemical Industry Monograph NO. 23, London. 1558-1563.

Flieder, Francoise. (1969). La Conservation des Documents Graphiques – Recherches Experimentales, Eyrolles, Paris.

Fosberg, Raymond F. and Sachet Marie-Helens. (1965). Manual for Tropical Herbaria, International Bureau of Plant Taxonomy and Nomenclature, Utrecht, Netherlands.

Frear, D.E.H. (1961) Pesticide Handbook, 13th Ed. College Science Pub. Pennsylvania.

Gaines, R.H. (1910). "Bacterial activity as a corrosive influence in the soil"., Ind. Eng. Chem, 2128-130.

Gallo, Fausta (1963) 'Biological Agents Which damage paper materials in Libraries and Archives, Recent Advances in Conservation, Ed. G. Thompson, Butterworths, London.

Gallo, Piero (1963). Problems in the use of Insecticides on occupied premises, Recent advances in Conservation, Ed. Thompson G. Butterworths, London.

Garrett, J.H (1891) The Action of Water on lead, London: H. K. Lewis.

Gilman, C. Joseph. (1957). A Mannual os Soil Fungi, Iowa State College Press, Ames, Iowa, U.S.A.

Gradidge, J.M.G. and Aitken A.D. (1967). Clothes Moths and Carpet Beetles, British Museum (N.H.) Economics series No. 14, London.

Grey, William D. (1959) The relation of Fungi to human affaires, Henry Holt and Co. Inc. New York.

Harder, E.C. (1919). Iron Depositing Bacteria and their Geologic Relations, Govt Printing office, Washington D.C.

Hardy, E. (1943). Fungi, moulds and mildews in Textiles, Rayon Textile Monthly, 24, pp. 138-140.

Harris, E. victor (1961) Termites - their recognition and control, John Wiley and Sone Inc. Nee York.

Hinton, H. E. (1945) A monograph of the Beetles associated with stored products, I, British Museum (N.N.)

Hocking, B. (1943) . Action against Anthrenus 'Wooly Bears' and what to do about them, Pest Control Pamphl. Ordn, Lab. 2, Cawnpore.

Hueck, H.J. (1964). Biodeterioration of Textiles and its prevention, Delft Conference on the Conservation of Textiles, I.I.C. , London.

Hueck, H.J. (1971) Biodeterioration and Environmental, Pollution, *Int . Biodetn.* Bull VI, VII, No. 2.

Hunt, G.M. and Garret, G.A. (1934) Wood Preservation, MeGraw Hill, New York.

Imms, A.D. (1957), A general Text Book of Entomology, Matheun, London.

Ingold, C.T. (1964). The Biology of Fungi, Hutchinson Ed. Ltd. London.

Inouve, Mayumi and Takao, Hiroyasu (1982) Studies om the Corrosion caused by micr-organisms in aircraft fuel tank of Alloy. Ibid.

Inoue, Mayumi (1982). Regeneration of Plastics by microorganisms, Papers related to microbial deterioration, Inoue Biodeterioration Laboratory, Japan.

Iverson, W.P. (1968). "Corrosion of iron and formation of iron phosphide by Desulfocibrio desulfuricans", Nature, 217, 1265-1267.

Iverson, P, Warren (1976) Mechanisms of microbial corrosion', Pest control operation, 3rd Edn., harvest Publ. Co.

Jedrzejewska, H. (1967) 'The damaging influence of disinfecting agents on sensitive ancient materials', I.I.C. Conference on Museum chimatology, London.

Johnston, R. Harmon, Smith, K. Virgil and Beal H. Raymond (1971) 'Chemicals for subterranean Temite Control: Resulte of long terms tests" Journal of Economic Entomology, Vol. 64, No. 3.

Kalshoven, L.G.E. (1935). Dermestiden in Nederlandsch *Indie Ent. Medm. Ned. Ind.* 1:4.

Kalshoven, L.G.E. (1938). De boekenoworm in Nederlandesh Indie *Ent. Med. Ned. Ind.* 4:1-2.

Keen, R. (1971) 'Controlling Algae and other growths on Concrete', Advisory Note, Cement and Concrete Assn. London.

Kingsolver, John (1981) 'Illustrated Guide to common Insect pests in Museumes', Applendix 'B' of pest control in Museums, Edwards R. Stephen *et. at.* Association of Systematics collections, U.S.A.

Kuritsyna, D.S. (1966) Protection of packing material against mold fungi during shipment of museum valuables, *Vestnik Moskovskogo Universiteta*

Moscow University) Herald, No. 6 Translated for F.S.T.C. by Techtram Corp.

Langwell W.H. (1958). The Conservation of Book and Documents, Pitman, London.

Lashen, E.S. (1971) 'New Method for evaluating antibaoterial activity directly on Fabric, *Applied Miorobiology,* Vol. 21 No.4.

Lehman, D. (1964) Conservation of Textiles at the West Berlin State Museum, *Stud* in *Conservation*, 9, 15.

Mallie, Arnold, Miller A.C. and Hill, R.C. (1959) 'The attraction of stains to three species of Fabric pests', Jour. of Economic Entomology, Vol. 52 No. 3.

Mallis, A. (1964) Handbook of Pest Control 4th Ed., Mc nair Dorland Co. New York.

Mc Keown (1944) as quoted by Szent Ivany (1968) Identification and control of Insect pests, The Conservation of Cultural property, Museums and Monument series, Unesco.

Metcalf, C.L. and Flint, W.P. (1939). Destructive and Useful Insects, Mc Grow Hill, New York.

Monro, H.A.U. (1960) Funigants and the residue problem, *Pest Control,* Vol. 28, No. 4.

Mori, Hachiro (1978) Insect pests of wooden cultural properties and their control in Japan, Conservation of Wood in Painting and the decoratives arts, contributions to the Oxford Congress, International Institute for conservation of Historic and Artistic Works.

Moyer W. John, (1953) Practical Taxidermy, Ronald Press Co. New York.

Mourier, Henri and Winding, Owe (1977) Collings guide to Wildlife in House and Home, Collins, London.

Mukerji, (1954). Indian Museum Notes, Indian Museum, Calcutta.

Nair, K.S.S. (1963) Observations on the biology of the Dermestid beetle, *Anthrenus vorax* Waterhouse under laborator conditions, *Jour. Anim. Morph.* and *Physiol.* 10:1.

Nair, K.S.S. (1964) Studies on certain aspects of the Physiology of the Furniture Carpet Beetle, *Anthremus Yorax* W. (Dermestidae, Coleoptera) Ph.D. Thesis, M.S. University of Baroda.

Nair, S.M. (1970). Studies on the Biodeterioration of Museum materials. Ph.D. thesis, M.S. University of Baroda.

Nair, S.M. (1971). 'Certain observations on the biodeterioration of Museum materials in India', Biodeterioration of Materials, Vol. II, Applied Science Publ., London.

Nair, S.M. (1972). 'Biodeterioration of Museum materials in tropical countries', Conservation in the Topics, International Centre for Conservation, Rome.

Nair, S.M. (1974). 'Evaluation of some common fungicides used for the protection of museum materials. Conservationof Cultural Property, Vol. II 1974, New Delhi.

Nair, S.M. (1975) Le ver des livres Indian (*Gastrallus indicus* Reitter), Zoo, 41 eme, No. 2, 1975, Brussels.

Niuksha, I.U.P. (1957) 'Microflora of Books and Paper' (In Russian) Bot. Zh. 41, 797-809, Prev, Det. Abstr, 15, PD.L. 30325.

Noon, Z.B.)1958). Food habits of the Khapra beetle lerva, Jour. Econ. Ent. 51:465.

Oldroyd, Harold (1970) Collecting preserving and studying Insects, Hutchinson Scientific and Technical, London.

Partridge, H.W. and Key G.E. (1949) 'Textile materiels:rot-proofing' J. Text. Inst, 40, 1077.

Patel, H.K. (1958). The Furniture Carpet Beetle (*Anthrenus Vorax* Waterhouse). Memoirs of the Ent. Soc. of India, No.6, 47 pp.

Paul, A. Dahm. (1957). Use of Radioisotopes in Pesticide Research, Advances in Pest Control Research, Vol. I, Ed. Metcalf, R.L. Interscience Pub. New York and London.

Pennel J.T., Retan, A.H. and Maxwell, R.V. (1970) Household insects and their control, Extension Bulletin 472, Washington State University, Pullman.

Petrova, G.I. (1964), 'Insects in Book store rooms and disinfestations measures', Collection of materials on the preservation of library resources. Translated from Russian by National Science Foundation, Washington, D.C.

Pillai, Parameswaran, P.R. (1957). Pests of stored fish and prawns. Bull. *Central Research Inst.* Ser. C. Natural Science, 5:3, 78 pp.

Plenderleith, H.J. (1957) and subsequent editions. The Conservation of Antiquities and works of Art, Oxford Univ. Press, London.

Plumbe, Wilfred J. (1964). The Preservation of Books in tropical and subtropical countries, Oxford Univ. Press. Kaula Lumpur, HongKong, London.

Prindle, B. (1935). The microbiology of Textile fibres, *Textile Res.* Vol. 5. pp. 542-568.

Pyenson, Louis. (1947). Pest control in the home garden Mc. Millan Co. New York.

Razumovskaya Z.P. and Mitushova, N.M. (1957) Observations on the formation of mould growths on optical glass *Optiko-Mekhan* Promyash, No. 3 Translated by P. Collins.

Rice, J.W. (1962) 'Principles of Textiles Conservation Science, No. 2, Practical Control of fungi and bacteria in fabric specimens', *Textile Museum Journal,* 1, 52-55.

Richard, T. Cotton, (1956). Pests of stored grain and grain products, Burgess Publ. Co. Minneapolie, U.S.A.

Roger, Heim, Fancolse Flieder and Niocot Nacqueline (1968) Combating moulds which develop on cultural property in tropical climates, The Conservation of Cultural property, Museums and Monument series, Unesco.

Roonwal, M.L. (1979) Termite Life and Termite control in Tropical south Asia, Scientific Publishers, Jodhpur, India.

Rosen Arthur (1962) 'Some Tips on residential Roach Control, *Pest Control,* June 1962.

Rowley, John (1943) Taxidermy and Museum Exhibition, Appleton, New York.

Royal Botanic Gardens, Kew (1953) Methyl Bromide as as fumigant for herbarium specimens, London.

Rybakova, S.G. (1964) Control of Mould fungi on books, Collection of materials on the preservation of library resources, translated from Russian by National Science foundation, Washington, D.C.

Shirk, Harold G. (1954) Optical Instruments and photographic equipment – in Deterioration of Materials by Greathouse and Wessel, Reinhold Publ. Corp. New York.

Skaife, S.H. (1955). Dwellers in darkness, Longmans, London.

Sohi, G.S. (1951) Bilogyof the Wooly Bear, *anthrenus Vorax Waterhouse, Proc. Nat. Acad. Sci. India* (B) 21:99.

Smith, George,(1969). An Introduction to Industrial Mycology, Sixth Ed. Edward Arnold Publ. London.

Smithers, Courtenary (1982) hand book of Insect collecting, David and Charless, Newton Aboot, London.

Snyder, E. Thomas and Zetek, James (1943) Effectiveness of Wood preservatives in preventing attack by Termites, U.S. Dept. of Agriculture, Circular 683.

St. George, R.A. Snyder, T.E. Dykstra W.W. and Henderson L.S. (1954). Biological Agents of Deterioration, Deterioration of Materials, Ed. Greathouse and Wessel, Reinhold Publ., New York.

Stoner J.H., Bear, N.S. and Indictor, N. (1975), Fungicidal Studies on canvas supports, Journal of Paint Technology. Vol. 4-7, No. 611.

Sviridova, A.I. and Syikovskaya (1957) Development of methods of protection of transparent optical components from mould growth, *Optiko Mekhan* Promyash, Vol. V.

Sykes, George (1965) Disinfection and Sterilization J.B. Lippincott C. Philadelphia.

Swezey (1933). Notes. Foreign subjects. (*Gastrallus laticollis*) – Proc. Hawaiin Ent. Soc. Honolulu 8:12, pp.237-238.

Szent-Ivany (1968) Identification and control of insect pests, The Conservation of Cultural Property, Museums and Monuments series, Unesco.

Tarshis, L.B.(1959). UCLA tests with desiccant dusts for roach control, *Pest Control* 27:6.

Taylor, Sir George (1962) as quoted by Fosberg and Sachet (1965) Manual for Tropical Herbaria, International Bureau for Flant Taxonomy and Nomenclature, Utrecht, Netherlands.

Thysen, A.C. and Bunker, H.J. (1924). studies on the bacterial decay of Textile fibres. I. Variations in the resistance of cottons of different regions to destruction by micro-organisms, Biochem. Jour. 18. pp.140-16.

Tonolo, Antonio and Giacobini Cleeia (1978) Microbiological changes in Frescoes, Recent Advances in Conservation Ed. G. Thompson, Butterworths, Londons.

Truman, C. Lee, Bennet W. Gray and Butts, L. Williams (1976) Pest Control Operations, 3rd Edn. Harvest Publ. Co.

United States Department of Agriculture (1953) 'Clothes Moths and Carpet Beetles: How to combat them' Home and Garden Bull, No. 24.

United States Department of Agriculture (1977), Sub-terranian Termites-their preservation and control in buildings, Home and garden Bulletin, 64.

Virginia Polytechnio Institute and State University, Extension Division (1972) 'Wood Infesting Beetles in the Home', Pub. 431.

Von Wolzogen Kuhr, C.A.H. and Vander Vlugt, L.S. (1934) De grafiteering Van gietijzer als electrobio-chemisch process in anaerobe gronden. Water 18(16) 147-165. (An English translation of this paper may be purchased from the Clearinghouse for Federal Scientific and Technical Information, U.S. Dept. of Commerce, Springfield, Virginia, U.S.A.

Wagstaffe, Reginald and Fidler, J. Havelock (1968). The Preservation of Natural History specimens Vol. II, H.F. & G. Witherly Ltd. London.

Waksman, Seman A. (1940) on Paper fungi as quoted by St. George, Snyder *et.al.* Greathouse and Wessel (1954) 'Biological Agents of Deterioration of materials, Reinhold Publ. New York.

Waterhouse, D.F. (1958) Wool digestion and mothproofing, Advances in Pest Control Research, Interscience Publishers, New Your.

Weis, H.W. and Caruthers, R.H. (1945) Insect enemies of books, New York. Public Library.

Werner, A.E. (1968). The Conservation of leather, wood bone and ivery and archival materials, The conservation of Cultural Property, Museums and Monuments, Series, Unesco.

Whitmore, T.C. (1965). 'Laurylpentachlorophenate protecting herbarium specimens' Taxon, 14. No. 5., 164-165.

Wigglesworth, V.C. (1953). The Principles of Insect Physiology, Methuen, London.

Willcocks, F.C.(1922) . A survey of the more important economic insects and mites of Egypt with notes on life-history, habits, natural enemies, and suggestions for control, Bull. *Agric. Sec. Cairo*, 1: 8: 483.

Winston, P.H. and Bates H. Donald, (1960). Saturated solutions for control of Humidity in Biological Research *Ecology*, 41:767.

INDEX

G

H

I

J

K

L